# BBC DOCTOR WHO

## THE OFFICIAL COOKBOOK

JOANNA FARROW

PHOTOGRAPHY AND PROP STYLING
HAARALA HAMILTON

BBC
BOOKS

# CONTENTS

# INTRODUCTION

How much the Doctor, or any Time Lord, actually needs to eat has never really been established. We know he likes jelly babies, and fish fingers and custard. He enjoys Sergeant Benton's coffee too, as well as good cheese and fine wine. But whether he really needs to eat and drink, or just enjoys the taste, is a mystery.

But whatever the truth, there is certainly plenty of food and drink in *Doctor Who*. And there's plenty of opportunity to turn some of the elements that have made *Doctor Who* so successful over the years into food and drink, too.

*Doctor Who: The Official Cookbook* is an inspiring collection of recipes, from simple snacks and teatime treats to spectacular centrepiece cakes. All things Whovian are included, from the Doctor's favourite foods (yes, there are some, whether he actually needs them or not), to the TARDIS and some iconic Who settings.

And of course, what *Doctor Who* cookbook would be complete without the monsters? Many of the Doctor's enemies don't need food – although some do like to feast on human flesh. The Cybermen simply re-energize themselves, while the Sontarans absorb pure energy through the probic vent on the back of their neck. The Zygons drink the milk of their Skarasen creatures, like the Loch Ness Monster. How – or if – the Daleks ingest is a mystery although we know they need static electricity… But what they all have in common is that – with the help of these recipes – each one can be made to taste so much better than they look!

You'll need little excuse to cook from your *Doctor Who* recipes. You might be looking for something fun and a bit different for a family supper, or simply fancy some tasty treats to nibble on as you watch the latest episode. Or why not push the TARDIS out and have a themed party?

The recipes vary considerably in their complexity. Some are easy enough for the kids and little Time Lords to help cook, like Fish fingers and Custard, Timey-Wimey Scones or Banana Party Pops. There's even the whole set of Doctors in the form of little iced biscuits. Hours of fun to be had decorating those! Others, like the Extermi-Cake and Sweet Silence require more patience and commitment, but even these are perfectly approachable.

Just make sure you have all the right ingredients for decoration. Allow time for cakes to cool before cutting them to shape and for the icing, where necessary, to set. Even if your finished result isn't quite cookbook perfect, it'll still look really impressive and set the scene for a memorable Whovian feast.

All you need to do then is invite a few Time Lords round and tuck in!

# SPEED OF LIGHT BITES

# ATRAXI SNAX

If Prisoner Zero – or any other prisoner come to that – escapes through a crack in time, then these are just the things to snack on while you hunt him down and threaten to destroy whole worlds. Breadsticks, homemade cheesey biscuits and hard-boiled eggs make up these tasty treats, perfect for a party snack or to share in the cabin of your pursuit ship. You could even try a mini version for smaller appetites using quails' eggs and wholemeal stick snacks. A bowl of spicy mayonnaise for dipping wouldn't go amiss either!

## MAKES 8 SNACKS

100g (3½oz) plain flour
75g (3oz) firm unsalted butter, cut into small pieces
1 medium egg yolk
100g (3½oz) Cheddar, grated, plus 3 tablespoons
a little beaten egg white
120g (4oz) pack of thin breadsticks
4 medium eggs, hard-boiled and shelled
4 blueberries
blue food colouring powder

**YOU WILL NEED:**
a fine paintbrush

**1** Preheat the oven to 200°C/400°F/gas 6. Line two baking sheets with baking parchment.

**2** Put the flour in a food processor and add the butter. Process until the mixture resembles coarse breadcrumbs. Add the egg yolk and 100g (3½oz) cheese and process to a smooth dough. Turn out onto the work surface and cut in half. Chill or freeze half the dough for making little biscuits another time (you only need half for this recipe). Shape the dough into a thick, short log, 12cm (5in) long.

**3** Cut the dough into eight slices and space the slices well apart on the baking sheets. Brush with beaten egg white.

**4** Break the breadsticks into varying lengths and press around the edges of each circle of dough. Make sure you press the ends in firmly so they'll be held in place as the dough cooks. Bake for 10 minutes until the dough is pale golden. Sprinkle the centres with the remaining 3 tablespoons cheese and return to the oven for a further 2 minutes to melt the cheese.

**5** While cooking, cut the ends off the hard-boiled eggs (this will leave a slice of about 5mm (¼in) in the centre to use up in a salad or sandwich). Press an end of egg onto each biscuit while the cheese is still soft. Leave to cool.

**6** Using a small teaspoon or the tip of a small sharp knife, make a small dip in the top of each egg. Halve the blueberries and place a half, cut-side face up, in each scooped out egg. Use a fine, dry paintbrush to paint the blue powder onto the breadsticks.

# CYBERMELTS

The walls of the Cybermen's city on the planet Telos are decorated with stylised images of Cybermen and sometimes just of Cyber heads. They're not made of toast, but you can achieve a similar effect on a plate. These make a great snack to munch on as you watch Doctor Who. Assemble the cheese shapes on the toast in advance, have the decorations ready to position and the snacks can be ready in a couple of minutes. You can also eat them untoasted, as shown here.

## FOR EACH CYBERMELT

1 slice Cheddar
1 slice Red Leicester
1 slice white or wholemeal bread, lightly toasted
a small piece of cucumber
1 radish
1 tbsp Hoisin sauce

**1** Trace the Cyber templates (see page 151) onto paper and cut out. Place the face-shaped template over the Cheddar slice and cut out with a knife. Cut out shapes from the Red Leicester cheese using the smaller templates.

**2** Position the face-shaped cheese on the toast and cut away the bottom half of the toast around the cheese. Cut out 5mm (¼in) strips from the remainder of the Cheddar slice and position one long strip across the top of the head and two smaller strips to finish halfway down the sides of the face. Position the pieces of Red Leicester cheese.

**3** Cut a thick slice of cucumber skin and cut out the shape for the top of the head and two corner pieces, as shown in the picture. Cut two small wedges of radish.

**4** To serve, preheat the grill to medium and very lightly toast the cheese until it's softened, watching closely to check that it doesn't melt and lose its shape. Spoon or pipe the Hoisin sauce into the eye and mouth areas and position the cucumber and radish to serve.

# KRILLITANE MONSTER MUFFINS

The Krillitanes are a composite species who absorb the characteristics and bits of the physical appearance of the races they conquer. So we can't be exactly sure what they look like at any given time… That also means that if your Krillitane doesn't look quite like the Krillitanes the Doctor encountered, then don't worry. It could still be a Krillitane. This savoury treat is made using two muffin sizes, assembled into one big Krillitane monster, perfect for a party so everyone can take whichever size muffin they fancy, or have room for. Kids would enjoy both the baking and decorating, so here's your chance to leave them to it.

## MAKES 9 LARGE MUFFINS AND 11 MINI MUFFINS

200g (7oz) frozen sweetcorn
100g (3½oz) streaky bacon, diced
175g (6oz) self-raising flour
150g (5oz) cornmeal
2 tsp baking powder
4 tbsp chopped coriander
2 medium eggs
200ml (7fl oz) milk
5 tbsp mild olive oil or sunflower oil

**TO FINISH:**
200g (7oz) smooth peanut butter
75g (3oz) ready-salted crisps (about 3 small bags)
120g (4oz) pack of thin breadsticks
1 small red onion
1 cherry tomato
1 slice of Cheddar
6 savoury crackers

**YOU WILL NEED:**
a 12-hole muffin tray with 7.5cm (3in) wide and 3cm (1¼in) deep paper cases, a 12-hole mini muffin tray with 4.5cm (1¾in) wide and 2cm (¾in) deep paper cases and a small paper piping bag or a polythene food bag

**1** Preheat the oven to 200°C/400°F/gas 6. Line 9 sections of a muffin tray with paper muffin cases. Line 11 sections of a mini muffin tray with mini muffin cases.

**2** Cook the sweetcorn in boiling water for 2 minutes, then drain. Heat a frying pan and fry the bacon for 5 minutes, stirring frequently, until golden.

**3** Combine the flour, cornmeal, baking powder and coriander in a bowl. Stir in the sweetcorn and bacon. Beat together the eggs, milk and oil and add to the bowl. Stir lightly until the ingredients are only just combined. Spoon into the paper cases, filling them almost full. Bake the smaller muffins for 10 minutes and the larger ones for 15 minutes. Leave to cool.

CONTINUES ON NEXT PAGE

SPEED OF LIGHT BITES

**4** Reserve 50g (2oz) of the peanut butter. Using a palette knife, spread the muffins with the remaining peanut butter. Arrange the muffins on a large tray or board, using the diagram (see page 153) to show how they're positioned. (The muffins used for the head will be positioned after sprinkling with the crisps).

**5** Half open the bags of crisps but leave the crisps inside. Crush the bags in your hands to crumble them as finely as you can. Sprinkle the crisps all over the muffins, filling the gaps between them. Press the breadsticks onto the limbs, hands and feet as shown. Cut small pieces of red onion and position on the hands and feet for claws. Rest the two 'head' muffins in position.

**6** Put the remaining peanut butter in a small paper piping bag or into one corner of a polythene food bag. Snip off a small tip. Pipe the outlines of the eyes and nostrils onto the head and sprinkle with a few more crisp crumbs. Cut small pieces of red onion and push into the eyes and nostrils. Add even smaller pieces of tomato for the centres of the eyes. Cut small ears and teeth from the cheese and press into the peanut butter. Position the crackers to represent wings.

"What you see is a simple morphic illusion. Scratch the surface and the *TRUE* *KRILLITANE* lies beneath."

# TIMEY-WIMEY WATCH SCONES

Both the Doctor and the Master have hidden their true essence and pretended to be human. It was such a good disguise even they didn't know who they really were! Both of them kept their real selves locked away inside a pocket watch. You probably can't keep a Time Lord's soul inside these scones, but they certainly look the part. The secret of most scone recipes is to roll the dough out thickly so the scones rise up during baking. This recipe is an exception to the rule as the dough should be rolled fairly thin for shaping the watch. Cook them briefly though or they'll overbake to a biscuit!

## MAKES 7 SCONES

225g (8oz) self-raising flour, plus extra for dusting
1 tsp baking powder
40g (1½oz) firm butter, cut into small pieces
50g (2oz) Cheddar, finely grated
150–175ml (5–6fl oz) milk
5 tbsp brown sauce
1½ tsp ground paprika
14 slices of Gouda
1 small carrot
½ small green pepper, seeded
100g (3½oz) cheese-flavoured potato hoops

**YOU WILL NEED:**
an 8cm (3in) and a 7cm (2¾in) plain round cutter, a paper piping bag or polythene food bag and a piping nozzle or small cutter

**1** Preheat the oven to 220°C/425°F/gas 7. Grease a large baking sheet. Put the flour and baking powder into a food processor and add the butter. Process until the mixture resembles fine breadcrumbs. Briefly process in the grated cheese. Add 150ml (5fl oz) of the milk and blend until the mixture comes together to form a soft dough, adding the remaining milk if the dough is dry.

**2** Tip out onto a floured surface and roll out to a 1cm (½in) thickness. Cut out rounds using an 8cm (3in) plain cutter. Roll out the dough trimmings to 5mm (¼in) thickness and cut out seven winders. Cut deep grooves into these and press against the sides of the scones, securing in place with a little milk. Bake for about 8 minutes until risen and turning pale golden. Transfer to a wire rack to cool.

**3** Carefully slice the top off each scone and reserve. Blend three tablespoons of the brown sauce with the paprika and put in a paper piping bag or spoon into one corner of a polythene food bag. Twist the open end to secure and snip off the smallest tip you can so the sauce can be piped in a fine line.

**4** Spread a little of the remaining brown sauce onto the cut side of each scone half. Cut out a 7cm (2¾in) circle from each of the cheese slices. Position one on each half of the scones to make watch bases and watch lids.

**5** Cut very thin slices of carrot and cut out small circles using the end of a piping nozzle or small cutter. Arrange two on each watch base. Pipe numerals onto each watch face and a border around the edges of the cheese circles using the piping bag. Cut fine shreds of green pepper and position for the watch hands.

**6** Snap the potato hoops in half. Position one piece against each winder and interlock the remainder together to create a watch chain effect.

# SONIC SCREWDRI-VEG

The Doctor's trusty Sonic Screwdriver has got him out of a lot of tight spots. He's used it to open locked doors, to explode landmines, even occasionally to undo screws. But he's never actually had to eat it. At least, not so far… Serve healthy vegetables in a fun way with these Sonic Screwdriver-shaped veggie kebabs. Lightly cooked with a little garlic butter, they're good on their own or with a meaty meal.

## MAKES 4 KEBABS

1 slender carrot
4 slender courgettes, at least 11cm (4¼in) long
4 medium mushrooms
25g (1oz) butter
1 small garlic clove, crushed
4 large pitted black olives, halved
8 frozen baby broad beans, thawed and skinned
salt and freshly ground black pepper

**YOU WILL NEED:**
4 bamboo skewers

**1** Peel the carrot, cut into four chunks and cook in boiling water for 5 minutes to soften. Add the courgettes and cook for 1 minute. Drain and cool slightly.

**2** Peel two courgettes and cut into four 5cm (2in) lengths. Make deep, lengthways grooves into the remaining courgettes (so they look stripy), and cut into four 5cm (2in) lengths. Cut four 2cm (¾in) lengths and eight 5mm (¼in) lengths from the carrots. Taper the thicker lengths at the ends. Cut four deep wedges out of each mushroom so you end up with a four-pronged shape. Cut four bamboo skewers down to 18cm (7in) lengths.

**3** Line a grill pan with foil. Melt the butter and mix with the garlic and a little seasoning.

**4** Thread each skewer as follows, pushing the vegetables down to the ends of the skewer:
thick piece of carrot, tapered end first
peeled length of courgette
thin piece of carrot
two olive halves, rounded ends touching
thin piece of carrot
striped length of courgette
mushroom, rounded-end first

**5** Preheat the grill to medium. Place the kebabs on the grill rack and brush with the garlic butter. Grill for 3–5 minutes, turning once until slightly softened. Thread two broad beans onto the tip of each skewer and serve hot.

# FISH FINGERS AND CUSTARD

Doctor Who tucked into the weird combination of frozen fish fingers and ready-made custard. Thankfully in this recipe, a rich cheese sauce takes the place of custard for dipping your delicious homemade fish fingers.

## SERVES 4

400g (14oz) piece skinned and boned cod or haddock fillet
1 tbsp plain flour
1 medium egg, beaten
75g (3oz) fresh breadcrumbs
oil for shallow frying

**FOR THE 'CUSTARD':**
15g (½oz) butter
15g (½oz) plain flour
300ml (½ pint) milk
1 tsp Dijon mustard
75g (3oz) mature Cheddar, grated
good pinch of ground turmeric
salt and freshly ground black pepper

**1** Cut the fish across into 2cm (¾in) wide fingers. Put the flour on a plate and season with a little salt and pepper. Put the egg on another plate and the breadcrumbs on a third. Dust the fish in the flour, then coat in beaten egg and finally in the breadcrumbs.

**2** For the custard, melt the butter in a small pan. Add the flour and cook over a gentle heat, stirring for 1 minute. Remove from the heat and gradually blend in the milk, whisking until smooth. Return to a gentle heat and cook, stirring continuously, until the sauce is thickened and smooth. Add the mustard, cheese and turmeric and cook for a further 2 minutes. Remove from the heat.

**3** Heat a 1cm (½in) depth of oil in a frying pan. Once hot enough (a sprinkling of breadcrumbs should sizzle when added to the pan), cook half the fish fingers for 4–5 minutes, turning once until golden. Drain on a plate lined with kitchen paper and keep warm while you cook the remainder.

**4** Reheat the cheese sauce gently and serve with the fish fingers.

# PASTA BOW TIE SALAD

As bow ties were the Eleventh Doctor's favourite accessory, this would surely be his favourite salad! And if you happen to have a spare Fez about the place that you can serve it in, then so much the better. The salad can be served warm or cold as a light meal on its own or as an accompaniment to chicken, pork or salmon.

## SERVES 4–5

2 red peppers, seeded and cut into small pieces
2 green peppers, seeded and cut into small pieces
5 tbsp olive oil
100g (3½oz) chorizo sausage, skinned and cut into small dice
25g (1oz) pine nuts
200g (7oz) dried pasta bows
2 tbsp capers, drained
15g (½oz) basil leaves, torn into pieces
a squeeze of lemon juice
salt

1. Preheat the oven to 200°C/400°F/gas 6. Scatter the peppers in a roasting tin and drizzle with two tablespoons of the oil. Bake for 30 minutes. Add the chorizo and pine nuts and bake for a further 30 minutes until the peppers are lightly browned.

2. Meanwhile, cook the pasta in a pan of plenty of boiling, lightly salted water for 12–15 minutes until tender. Drain and transfer to a bowl.

3. If serving warm, stir the baked peppers, pine nuts and chorizo, capers, basil, lemon juice and remaining oil into the pasta. Stir well to combine. If serving cold, leave the pasta to cool before stirring in the remaining ingredients.

"Bow ties ARE COOL"

# MUNCHIE MIRE WARRIOR

Although Odin's formidable looking Mire warriors appear tricky to make, they're actually not as hard to create as they are to fight off if they attack your village. You can shape and bake the warrior in advance and reheat it, covered with foil, to freshen it up. It also freezes well.

## MAKES 1 BREAD

250g (9oz) plain wholemeal flour
250g (9oz) self-raising white flour, plus extra for dusting
½ tsp bicarbonate of soda
1 tsp salt
4 tbsp olive oil
275ml (9½fl oz) buttermilk
2–4 tbsp milk
2 thin breadsticks
1 tbsp HP sauce or Hoisin sauce

**1** Preheat the oven to 200°C/400°F/gas 6. Grease a large baking sheet. Put the flours, bicarbonate of soda, salt and olive oil in a bowl. Add the buttermilk and two tablespoons of the regular milk and mix to a dough with a round-bladed knife. Add the remaining milk if the dough feels dry. Turn out onto the work surface and knead into a smooth ball.

**2** Take 150g (5oz) of the dough and shape into a flat cone shape. Place on the centre of the baking sheet with the thin end towards you for the body. Take 225g (8oz) dough and shape into a thick wedge (like a wedge of cheese). Position for the head so the thin end rests over the body. Shape two 75g (3oz) sausage shapes and press into position either side of the body so the shoulders come almost halfway up the sides of the head. Shape another 50g (2oz) sausage of dough and add to the end of the monster's left arm. Add a 20g (¾oz) piece of dough to the end of the other arm. For the right hand, take a 20g (¾oz) ball of dough and cut slits into one side with a knife. Pinch out into claws and press into position.

CONTINUES ON NEXT PAGE

**3** Shape two 40g (1½oz) sausage shapes of dough and position for the tops of the legs. Add 15g (½oz) pieces to the ends for the lower legs and small pieces for the feet. Push two lengths of breadstick into the monster's left arm to resemble the gun. Press deep diagonal grooves into the trunk of the body to define the ribs.

**4** Thinly roll out the remaining dough on a lightly floured surface. From this cut out all the armour pieces as shown in the picture and position on the centre of the body, across the upper arms, upper legs and right lower arm. Roll tiny balls of the remaining dough and position at intervals around the armour plates. If they don't easily stick in place, brush the dough with milk first.

**5** Bake for 35–45 minutes until slightly risen and deeper in colour. Using the tip of a sharp knife, cut a thin slit across the top of the head, then use a small teaspoon (or piping bag) to pipe the HP or Hoisin sauce into the slit.

# "THE MIRE ARE COMING

## for each and every one of you. So what you going to do?"

# OOD HEAD BREAD

The Ood might look rather revolting with their squid-like tendrils, but they can be delicious in bread form if properly baked. This is a fun family bread to make – mildly spiced and tomatoey at one end and plain at the other. Don't worry too much about the shaping. If you get the eyes, ears and tendrils in the right place, it'll look incredibly 'Ood' like. If you've any dough leftover, shape it into balls and bake as mini bread rolls. Like most breads, this one freezes well too if you're planning a Doctor Who party and want to get ahead. Then all you need for your party are a few obliging Oods to hand out the drinks.

## MAKES 1 LARGE LOAF

1kg (2¼lb) strong white bread
    flour, plus extra for dusting
1 tbsp easy-blend yeast
1 tbsp salt
4 tbsp olive oil
about 600ml (1 pint) warm water
2 tsp ground paprika
1 tbsp sun-dried tomato paste
1 tsp yeast extract paste
2 blueberries

**YOU WILL NEED:**
a 5cm (2in) plain round cutter and
a paintbrush

**1** Put the flour, yeast, salt, oil and almost all of the water in a large bowl and mix with a round-bladed knife to make a soft dough. Add the rest of the water if the dough feels dry and crumbly. Turn out onto a floured surface and knead for 10 minutes or until smooth and elastic. Return to a clean bowl and cover with cling film. Leave in a warm place for about 1 hour or until doubled in size.

**2** Turn the dough out onto the work surface and cut off a third. Knead the paprika and tomato paste into the smaller portion on a floured surface. It'll become very sticky while you knead in the tomato paste, but will gradually become smooth and more manageable.

**3** Grease a large baking sheet. Reserve 300g (11oz) of the plain dough and shape the remainder into an egg shape for the Ood's head. Place on the baking sheet so the pointed end of the dough is in one corner of the baking sheet, giving you plenty of room to assemble the rest of the Ood diagonally across the baking sheet.

**4** Pull off a small piece of the tomato-flavoured dough and roll it into a long thin sausage under the palms of your hands until about 25cm (10in) long. Push down onto the main section of the head on the baking sheet so it overlaps by 6–8cm (2½–3in). Curl the other end down towards the corner of the baking sheet. Make more tendrils in the same way, varying their length and thickness. You might not need all the tomato-flavoured dough.

CONTINUES ON NEXT PAGE ▶

**5** Take 75g (3oz) of the reserved plain dough and cut in half. Roll under the palms of your hands into two thin sausages, each about 10cm (4in) long. Position one on each side of the tendrils so the two tips meet at the nose end and the other ends are tucked under the bread. Secure in place with a dampened paintbrush.

**6** Preheat the oven to 200°C/400°F/gas 6. To finish the face, use large scissors to make deep snips into the dough about a third of the way up the sides of the face for ears. Take a ball of dough, about the size of a large tomato, and stretch into an oblong. Push down into the dough above the tendrils. Roll more dough under the palms of your hands to about a 1cm (½in) thickness. Cut off a 4cm (1½in) piece and press down into the dough across the base of the piece you've just added. Cut more strips, making each slightly wider than the previous, and position across the face until slightly higher than the level of the ears. Use the tip of a knife to score the area above the tendrils.

**7** For the eyes, flatten more dough to a 5mm (¼in) thickness on the surface and cut out a circle with a 5cm (2in) plain round cutter. Cut into two semicircles. Press into the dough near the ears for the undersides of the eyes. Shape and position two thin strips of dough for the tops of the eyes.

**8** Bake the bread for 25 minutes until risen and just firm. While baking, blend the yeast extract with a dash of water to thin the consistency. Brush over the face in and around the eyes, ears and central area. Return to the oven for a further 5–10 minutes until cooked through. Leave to cool on the baking sheet. Once cool, push a blueberry into the centre of each eye.

# "WE MUST FEED.... you — if you are hungry."

# SLITHEEN CUISINE

The Slitheen from the planet Raxacoricofallapatorius are one of the scarier Doctor Who monsters of recent years. You probably won't be able to reproduce the 'gas emissions' they make when pretending to be human, but choose an assortment of knobbly potatoes to bake and you'll be halfway there to making a rather impressive-looking Slitheen in its true, ugly form. Do make sure you leave the potatoes for about 15 minutes after baking so they're not too hot to handle, then you'll be able to squidge and mould them into shape. One Slitheen will serve three to four as part of a meal, but you could make two batches for a larger gathering.

## MAKE 1 SLITHEEN

1 large baking potato, about
    400g (14oz)
1 small baking potato, about
    200g (7oz)
6 new potatoes in various sizes
1 tbsp olive or vegetable oil
3 large black olives, pitted
100g (3½oz) full-fat cream cheese
1 tbsp green pesto
6 whole, small Guindilla peppers
    from a jar
a small piece of pitta bread
1 slice Red Leicester
salt

**YOU WILL NEED:**
a paper piping bag or polythene
food bag

**1** Preheat the oven to 200°C/400°F/gas 6. Pierce all the potatoes with a fork and rub with the oil. Sprinkle lightly with salt to season. Put the large potato in a small roasting tin and bake for 20 minutes, then add the medium potato and bake for 30 minutes. Add the new potatoes and bake for a further 30–40 minutes until all the potatoes are tender. Leave until cool enough to handle.

**2** Push the large potato down on a board using your thumbs to mould it into a body that sits upright. Transfer to a serving plate or board. Cut a thick slice off the thickest end of the small baking potato and reserve. Push in the sides of the potato with your fingers to shape the head. Use the tip of a knife to push a small mouth shape into the potato. You should be able to pinch the potato above the mouth to shape a small nose. Cut a slither of olive and push it into the mouth. Cut two large rounds from the ends of the olives and secure in place with a dab of cream cheese to make the eyes.

CONTINUES ON NEXT PAGE

**3** Mix the remaining cream cheese with the pesto. Cut a cube shape from the piece of potato you've sliced off and position this on top of the body. Spoon the cream cheese into a paper piping bag (or one corner of a polythene food bag). Twist the bag to secure the cream cheese in place and cut off a small tip. Pipe around the cube of potato to form a wrinkly neck. Position the head on top. If the head feels insecure, push a wooden cocktail stick down through the head and neck and into the body to hold it in shape.

**4** Assemble the new potatoes on either side of the body to shape the long, gangly arms, starting with the lower arm sections on the board and building up the sections either side of the body. Squidge them together to hold them in place. For the potatoes that are either side of the shoulders, cut a small slice off so they sit snugly against the body. Secure in place if necessary with a dab of cream cheese. Cut long tips off the peppers to resemble claws and position at the ends of the arms.

**5** For the neck gadget, cut a 2 x 1cm (¾ x ½in) rectangle of pitta bread. Cut a 1cm (½in) square from the cheese (cut out the centre if you can) and secure to the bread with a dab of cream cheese. Push gently into position at the neck.

# "Have you got ANY VINEGAR?"

# THE DOCTOR'S BLACKBOARD

The Twelfth Doctor likes his blackboard. He often jots down ideas or theories or strange symbols that probably make no sense at all to anyone else in the universe. To make this recipe look really effective, use a square or rectangular shallow baking dish with a rim to serve as the frame of the blackboard. Delicious on its own as a veggie supper, it also makes a tasty partner to chicken, lamb, sausages or white fish.

## SERVES 4–6

4 large aubergines
100ml (3½fl oz) olive oil
2 medium onions, chopped
1 fennel bulb, chopped
3 garlic cloves, crushed
2 x 400g (14oz) tins chopped
    tomatoes
1 tsp dried oregano
1 tsp caster sugar
150g (5oz) piece of rindless firm
    goat's cheese
75g (3oz) Parmesan, grated
5 tbsp ready-made cheese sauce
salt and freshly ground black
    pepper

**YOU WILL NEED:**
a shallow square or rectangular
baking dish with a rim and a
polythene food bag

**1** Preheat the oven to 190°C/375°F/gas 5. Line two baking sheets with baking parchment.

**2** Holding an aubergine vertically on the chopping board, cut a long, thick slice of skin from one side. Cut off about four more thick slices (set them aside) so you're left with the fleshy, skin-free centre. Cut this into thick slices. Repeat with the remaining aubergines. Place all the 'fleshy' aubergine slices in a single layer on the baking sheets and brush lightly with olive oil. Turn the slices over and brush with more oil. Season with a little salt and pepper and bake for 45 minutes, turning once halfway through cooking.

**3** Heat the remaining oil in a large pan and gently fry the onions and fennel for 6–8 minutes until softened and beginning to colour. Stir in the garlic, then the tomatoes, oregano, sugar and a little seasoning. Cook gently for 25 minutes, stirring occasionally, until the sauce is thick and pulpy.

**4** Cut a cylindrical shape from the firm centre of the goat's cheese to resemble a piece of chalk. Dice the remaining goat's cheese.

CONTINUES ON NEXT PAGE ▶

# "RUN, YOU CLEVER BOY and be a DOCTOR."

**5** Set aside all the aubergine skin slices. Place half the baked 'fleshy' aubergine slices in the base of a shallow square or rectangular baking dish with a rim. Spread half the tomato sauce on top and sprinkle with half the Parmesan cheese. Add the remaining baked 'fleshy' aubergine slices, then the rest of the tomato sauce and Parmesan. Scatter the diced goat's cheese on top. Finally, add the aubergine skin slices, if necessary cutting and patching together the slices so the filling is completely covered.

**6** Cover the surface of the dish with foil, pressing it down firmly to flatten the filling. If you have a small metal baking dish that fits snugly inside the rim of the larger dish, position it on top and fill with baking beans. This will help keep the surface of the 'blackboard' flat. Bake for 30 minutes.

**7** Heat the cheese sauce either in a small bowl in the microwave or in a small pan and stir until smooth. Leave to cool slightly and spoon into one corner of a polythene food bag. Twist the bag to contain the sauce and snip off the tip. Use the sauce to 'scribble' words or symbols over the 'blackboard'. Add the goat's cheese 'chalk' and serve.

# A PIZZA CASSANDRA

The Lady Cassandra O'Brien Dot Delta Seventeen may have had hundreds of cosmetic operations to achieve that perfect flat figure of hers, but you can achieve a similar result with some ready-made puff pastry – a great base for a cheesey pizza topping. It's so easy to shape the scalloped edge to resemble Cassandra, stretched in her silver frame and all the more effective if you serve it in a ridged aluminium or stainless steel baking tray. Just don't let her dry out, or cracks may appear…

## SERVES 4

500g (1lb 2oz) pack of puff pastry
plain flour, for dusting
1 red pepper, seeded
2 tbsp olive oil
1 onion, chopped
400g (14oz) tin chopped tomatoes
½ tsp dried oregano
3 tbsp tomato ketchup
350g (12oz) ready-made cheese
   sauce
100g (3½oz) Gruyère
1 cucumber slice, halved
1 black grape
salt and freshly ground black pepper

**YOU WILL NEED:**
a 10–11cm (4–4¼in) plain round cutter

**1** Preheat the oven to 200°C/400°F/gas 6. Grease a large aluminium or stainless steel baking sheet or tray, preferably ridged.

**2** Roll out the pastry on a lightly floured surface to a rectangle measuring about 38 x 30cm (15 x 12in) or as big as your baking sheet will contain. Using a 10–11cm (4–4¼in) plain round cutter, cut out two scalloped edges from one short side of the rectangle and three from each long side. Use a knife to cut off one long curve from the remaining short end. This will be the base. Slice off the corners.

**3** Transfer the pastry to the baking sheet. Use the tip of the knife to cut a shallow groove all around the edges of the pastry, about 1cm (½in) in from the edges. Prick the base with a fork and bake for 20 minutes until puffed and golden. Flatten the risen centre down with the back of a spoon.

**4** For Cassandra's face, cut a mouth from the red pepper, making it about 5cm (2in) wide and 2.5cm (1in) tall at the widest point. Put to one side and dice the remaining red pepper.

**5** Heat the oil in a pan and fry the onion and chopped pepper for 5 minutes to soften. Stir in the tomatoes, oregano and a little seasoning. Bring to the boil, reduce the heat and simmer gently for 10 minutes, stirring frequently, until thick and pulpy. Leave to cool.

**6** Stir the ketchup into the tomato sauce and spread into the pastry case in an even layer. If the cheese sauce is thick, give it a good stir to loosen it up. Spread in an even layer over the tomato base. Grate the cheese on top.

**7** Bake the pizza for 25 minutes or until the cheese is melted and bubbling, but not turning brown. Position the red pepper mouth and two semicircles of cucumber for eyes. Cut two slices of grape, then cut a thin slice off each and position in the centre of the cucumber pieces. Leave to stand for 15 minutes before serving to let the sauce cool and thicken a little. Serve with a leafy salad.

# ZYGON PIE

As we know, the Zygons are already here. Anyone could be a Zygon as they can disguise themselves to blend into human society. Though they probably wouldn't disguise themselves as a tasty pie! This is a delicious sausage and vegetable pie wrapped in a puff pastry case, though the decoration of the pie resembles the reddish, reptilian, suckered skin of the Zygon monster. All you need to accompany it is a leafy salad.

## SERVES 6–8

750g (1lb 10oz) sweet potatoes, scrubbed, cut into small cubes
2 large red onions, roughly chopped
2 tbsp olive oil
2 garlic cloves, chopped
500g (1lb 2oz) lean sausage meat
1 tsp dried oregano
3 tsp sun-dried tomato paste
2 x 500g (1lb 2 oz) packs of puff pastry
plain flour, for dusting
1 medium egg yolk
freshly ground black pepper

**1** Preheat the oven to 190°C/375°F/gas 5. Grease a large baking sheet. Scatter the sweet potato cubes in a roasting tin with the onion. Drizzle with the oil and roast for 45 minutes until the potatoes are tender, turning the ingredients once during cooking. Add the garlic and roast for a further 5 minutes. Leave to cool.

**2** Put the sausage meat into a bowl with the oregano, two teaspoons of the tomato paste and plenty of freshly ground black pepper. Mix well.

**3** Roll out each block of pastry on a lightly floured surface to a 35 x 30cm (14 x 12in) rectangle. Cut out a 30 x 25cm (12 x 10in) oval shape from one piece and transfer to the baking sheet. Reserve the trimmings. Cut out a slightly larger oval shape from the other rectangle. This should measure about 33 x 28cm (13 x 11in). Brush the edges of the pastry oval on the baking sheet with water. Arrange the sweet potato mixture over the pastry, leaving a 2cm (¾in) rim of pastry around the edges. Distribute the sausage meat mixture on top, doming it up slightly in the centre. Position the second pastry oval on top, pressing it down firmly around the edges and trimming off any excess pastry.

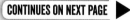 CONTINUES ON NEXT PAGE ▶

**4** In a small bowl, mix together the remaining tomato paste, the egg yolk and 1 teaspoon water. Brush sparingly over the surface of the pie. Use the tip of a knife to mark a shallow line right down the centre, without cutting right through to the filling. Roll out the pastry trimmings and cut out twenty-four 7.5 x 1cm (3 x ½in) strips. Brush lightly with the egg mixture. Fold each strip into three layers. Press twenty of these around the edges of the pie, spacing slightly apart and pushing firmly in place to secure. Position the remaining four over the top half of the marked line down the pie centre.

**5** Using the tip of the knife, cut the outline of the slitty eyes, nostrils and mouth onto the pastry. Cut further lines either side of the central decorations over the skull area of the pastry.

**6** Bake for 30 minutes. Brush the pie with more of the egg mixture over the 'dark' areas of the Zygon face. These include the eyes, nostrils and mouth, around the tubes and over the skull area of the face. Return to the oven for a further 30 minutes until deep golden, covering with foil if the pastry over browns. Leave to stand for 10 minutes before serving.

> **"I shall recreate MY OWN PLANET, here on EARTH."**

# WHO-GAZY HANDMINES

If you were trapped in a field of handmines, it would be great if you could just eat your way out. Of course, the young Davros didn't have that option and had to rely on the Doctor to save him. Or not. A lovely potato-topped family fish pie makes an effective base for that handmine scene and is like a stargazy fish pie, except this one has hand shapes instead of fish heads sticking out of it. Black seeds such as sesame, nigella and mustard add a dark and mysterious 'earthiness'.

## SERVES 4–5

500g (1lb 2oz) white fish, such as cod, haddock, pollack, skinned weight
3 tbsp milk
4 medium eggs, soft-boiled and shelled
12 large fresh or frozen peeled raw prawns
900g (2lb) floury potatoes
50g (2oz) butter
1 tbsp mild olive or vegetable oil
1 fennel bulb, chopped
3 tbsp chopped dill
300ml (½ pint) ready-made cheese sauce
50g (2oz) Cheddar, grated
2 tbsp nigella seeds, mustard seeds or black sesame seeds
salt and freshly ground black pepper

**YOU WILL NEED:**
a 9cm (3½in) hand cookie cutter

**1** Check over the fish for any bones. Put in a frying pan, add the milk and a little seasoning and cover with a lid. Cook gently for 10 minutes or until the fish is just cooked. Transfer to a pie dish, flaking the fish into chunky pieces. Tuck the whole eggs between the fish chunks and scatter with the prawns.

**2** Cut five or six 1cm- (½in-) thick slices from the largest potatoes and stamp out hand shapes using a 9cm (3½in) hand cookie cutter. Set aside. Cut the trimmings and the rest of the potatoes into chunks and cook in a pan of boiling, lightly salted water for 12 minutes until tender. Drain and return to the pan. Mash well and stir in 25g (1oz) of the butter and a little seasoning.

**3** Preheat the oven to 190°C/375°F/gas 5. Melt the remaining butter with the oil in a frying pan and gently fry the potato hand shapes for 5 minutes, turning once, until pale golden. Lift out onto a plate and gently fry the fennel for 5 minutes to soften. Stir in the dill and scatter into the pie dish. Spoon the cheese sauce on top. Spoon the mash over the sauce and spread roughly with a fork. Sprinkle with the cheese.

**4** Sprinkle the hand shapes with some of the seeds. Bake the pie for 15 minutes. Remove from the oven and push the potato hands into the top of the pie so they stand upright. Scatter with the remaining seeds and bake for a further 30–40 minutes until the surface is bubbling and golden. Serve with peas.

"Survival is just **A CHOICE.** Choose it **NOW.** "

# 'INSIDE A DALEK' SALAD

The Doctor once described the Dalek creature inside the casing as 'a living, bubbling lump of hate'. For many years the actual Dalek creature wasn't shown in full on television – just a claw here or a glimpse of something nasty there. But now we know what the Dalek creature looks like, and here's how you can make your own, although it won't actually be living or bubbling. With a little imagination, a tasty salad or lunchbox can be made to resemble the grossest matter inside a Dalek. Vegetable ribbons, noodles, some tendrilly squid and dyed eggs really do work well and taste so good. Try to forget the inspiration behind this dish when you eat it!

## SERVES 2

2 tbsp red or white wine vinegar
2 tsp blue food colouring
4 medium eggs
4 spring onions
50g (2oz) wholewheat noodles
2 courgettes
2 carrots
100g (3½oz) ready-made squid or octopus salad (optional)
4 tbsp mayonnaise
1 small garlic clove, crushed
good pinch of chilli powder
1 tsp soy sauce

**1** Put the vinegar and food colouring in a small pan with 700ml (1¼ pints) water and bring to a gentle simmer. Add the eggs and cook gently for 4 minutes. Lift the eggs out on a spoon and run under cold water so they're cool enough to handle. Using the back of a teaspoon, gently crack each egg all over so the shells are shattered, but not falling apart. Return to the pan and simmer for a further 2 minutes. Turn off the heat and leave the eggs to cool in the liquid, then remove the shells.

**2** Trim and cut the spring onions lengthways into thin strips. Bring a small pan of water to the boil, add the spring onion strips and cook for 30 seconds. Lift out with a slotted spoon into a bowl and add the noodles to the pan. Cook gently until tender. Drain thoroughly and add to the bowl.

**3** Shape the courgettes and carrots into ribbons. An inexpensive spiral cutter is ideal for this. If you don't have one, coarsely grate the vegetables or use the shredder attachment of a food processor. Add to the bowl with the squid or octopus salad, if using. Bury the shelled eggs into the salad.

**4** Combine the mayonnaise, garlic, chilli powder and soy sauce in a small bowl. Dot over the salad and combine very lightly so the salad looks a bit gooey in places.

# PICNIC AT ASGARD

No records survive of exactly what the Doctor and River Song had to eat when they went on their picnic at Asgard. It is also not entirely clear if this was the Asgard of Norse mythology, one of the Nine Worlds and home to the Aesir gods, or whether it was the Asgard crater on Jupiter's moon Callisto. The crater seems more likely, but with the Doctor and River you never quite know. But whatever they ate, and wherever they were, you can be sure they would have loved this delicious pie.

## SERVES 8

500g (1lb 2oz) pack of puff pastry
plain flour, for dusting
1 tsp vegetable oil
1 onion, chopped
800g (1¾lb) skinless, boneless
   chicken breasts, cut into large
   chunks
1 tsp dried oregano
1 tsp fennel seeds, crushed
1 tsp salt
500g (1lb 2oz) cooked ham, in
   one piece, about 2cm (¾in)
   thick
beaten egg, to glaze
freshly ground black pepper

**YOU WILL NEED:**
a loaf tin with base measurements
of 18 x 9cm (7 x 3½in), baking
beans or lentils or dried beans
reserved for baking blind, a 5cm
(2in) heart-shaped cutter and a
meat thermometer, if you have one

**1** Preheat the oven to 200°C/400°F/gas 6. Thinly roll out 350g (12oz) of the pastry on a lightly floured surface and use to line the base and sides of a loaf tin with base measurements of 18 x 9cm (7 x 3½in). The pastry should come up the sides of the tin and overhang the edges by at least 3cm (1¼in) to allow for it to shrink back. Press the pastry firmly up the sides and into the corners, squeezing the creases in the pastry firmly into the ends of the tin.

**2** Line the pastry with foil, pushing it firmly into the corners, up the sides and over the top edges of the tin. The foil will hold the pastry in place as it bakes. Fill the base with baking beans (you can also use lentils or dried beans reserved for baking blind). Bake for 30 minutes. Remove the foil and beans and press the pastry back against the sides of the tin. Reduce the oven temperature to 160°C/325°F/gas 3.

**3** For the filling, heat the oil in a small frying pan and fry the onion for 5 minutes to soften. Transfer to a bowl. Finely chop the chicken in a food processor. Add to the bowl with the oregano, fennel and salt. Season with black pepper and mix well.

**4** Using a 5cm (2in) heart-shaped cutter, cut shapes out of the ham. Cut the shapes close together so you have enough hearts and don't waste too much ham. If the cutter is hard to press through the ham, tap it gently with a rolling pin.

CONTINUES ON NEXT PAGE ▶

"Life with a **TIME TRAVELLER.** Never knew it could be such **HARD WORK.**"

**5** Press half the chicken mixture into the pastry-lined tin and push a deep groove along the centre of the chicken. Press the heart shapes down into the groove in the chicken filling, packing them closely one behind the other right down the length of the tin. Spoon the remaining chicken mixture around the sides and over the top of the ham.

**6** Trim off the excess pastry around the top of the tin, leaving enough of a pastry rim to support the lattice decoration. Brush the pastry edges with beaten egg. Thinly roll out the remaining pastry and cut into 1.5cm- (⅝in-) wide strips. Use to make a lattice decoration over the top of the pie. Brush the top with more beaten egg.

**7** Bake for 1½ hours or until the pastry is golden and the chicken feels firm when you push a skewer down into it. Use a meat thermometer if you have one. It should register at least 82°C (180°F). Leave the pie in the tin to firm up and serve warm or cold in thick slices.

# THE IMPOSSIBLE GIRL'S IMPOSSIBLE RECIPE

Clara, 'the impossible girl', strived to cook a baked soufflé. Although she didn't know it, she had been turned into a Dalek at the time, which probably explains her rather limited success and why we saw her tipping a failed attempt into the bin! Hot soufflés have a reputation for being difficult because a light touch is needed to keep the mixture aerated and, of course, they sink so quickly after baking. Fingers crossed that this delicious raspberry soufflé will not only be possible, but perfect!

## SERVES 6

butter, for greasing
100g (3½oz) caster sugar, plus
    extra for coating
2 tsp cornflour
250g (9oz) fresh or frozen
    raspberries
squeeze of lemon juice
4 medium egg whites
icing sugar, for dusting
pouring cream, to serve

**YOU WILL NEED:**
six 150ml (¼ pint) individual
soufflé dishes

**1** Thoroughly grease six 150ml (¼ pint) individual soufflé dishes with the butter. Sprinkle a little caster sugar over the butter, tilting the dishes so they're evenly coated in sugar. Chill.

**2** Mix the cornflour in a pan with 2 tablespoons water. Add the raspberries and lemon juice and slowly bring to a simmer, crushing the raspberries with the edge of the spoon and stirring until the mixture has thickened slightly. Press through a sieve into a bowl, scraping the mixture from the underside of the sieve so you don't waste any.

**3** Preheat the oven to 180°C/350°F/gas 4. Whisk the egg whites in a thoroughly clean bowl until softly peaking. Gradually whisk in the remaining caster sugar, a spoonful at a time, until thick and glossy. Spoon a quarter of the meringue over the raspberries and fold in gently with a large metal spoon to lighten it. Fold in the remainder.

**4** Divide the mixture among the dishes and level the tops. Place on a baking sheet and bake for 20 minutes. Dust lightly with icing sugar and serve immediately with pouring cream.

# EGGS-STIR-MIX-BAKE

(SAY IT FAST AND LIKE A DALEK...)

# EXTERMI-CAKE

The Daleks may be the most evil and ruthless life form in the universe, but with a bit of care and effort, a Dalek can also be made into a delicious and impressive cake. Ideally, make the sponge cake a day in advance so it can firm up a little before cutting and shaping.

## SERVES 12–15

5 small, very ripe bananas
300g (11oz) unsalted butter, softened
300g (11oz) light muscovado sugar
4 medium eggs, beaten
2 tsp vanilla extract
400g (14oz) self-raising flour

### TO FINISH:

175g (6oz) unsalted butter, softened
250g (9oz) icing sugar, plus extra for dusting
1 tsp vanilla extract
150g (5oz) grey ready-to-roll icing
1kg (2¼lb) white ready-to-roll icing, coloured a pale, warm brown with a mix of brown and yellow paste food colourings
edible gold food spray
150g (5oz) black ready-to-roll icing
silver food colouring
3 candy sticks
small bit of yellow ready-to-roll icing

### YOU WILL NEED:

a 1.5 litre (2½ pint) and a 400ml (14fl oz) ovenproof bowl, a 23cm (9in) round cake board, a 10cm (4in) plain round cutter and a fine paintbrush

**1** Preheat the oven to 160°C/325°F/gas 3. Grease a 1.5 litre (2½ pint) and a 400ml (14fl oz) ovenproof bowl and line the bases with circles of baking parchment. Cut a long strip of baking parchment measuring 55 x 15cm (22 x 6in) and fold in half lengthways. Fit around the top of the large bowl so the paper extends the rim by 4cm (1½in). Secure the overlap in place with tape or a paper clip and grease the inside of the paper collar. (The collar will prevent the cake mixture spilling over the top of the bowl as it bakes).

**2** Mash the peeled bananas in a small bowl. Beat together the butter and muscovado sugar in a large bowl until pale and creamy. Gradually beat in the eggs, a little at a time. Stir in the bananas and vanilla. Add half the flour and fold in gently with a large metal spoon. Fold in the remainder. Spoon 1kg (2¼lb) of the mixture into the large bowl and the rest into the smaller bowl. Bake the small bowl for 45 minutes and the large one for 1¼ hours. The cakes are cooked when they feel firm and a skewer inserted in the centre comes out clean. Leave to cool in the bowls for 15 minutes.

**3** Loosen the edges of the cakes with a knife and turn out onto a wire rack to cool completely. Beat together the butter, icing sugar and vanilla extract until pale and creamy. Position the cakes with their flat tops face down on the surface. Using a sharp knife, trim the sides off the small cake so they're straight rather than curved. Trim the sides off the larger cake in the same way. The diameter of the cake base should be about 13cm (5in). Cut the small cake vertically in half and the larger cake into three. Sandwich all the layers back together using most of the buttercream. Re-assemble the layers so the cake is almost vertical on one side (this will form the back of the Dalek) and sloping at the front. Secure the small cake on top of the large with a little more buttercream. Spread the remaining buttercream all over the cake.

CONTINUES ON NEXT PAGE ▶

**4** Dampen a 23cm (9in) round cake board with water. Thinly roll out the grey icing on a surface dusted with icing sugar and lay the icing over the board. Smooth out with the palms of your hands and trim off the excess around the edges.

**5** For the domed top of the Dalek, take 150g (5oz) of the brown-coloured icing and knead into a smooth ball. Flatten out on a lightly dusted surface until 10cm (4in) in diameter. To get a really neat edge, flatten the icing out to a slightly larger round and cut through with a 10cm (4in) round cutter. Position on top of the cake and ease slightly down the sides. Spray with a little edible gold spray.

**6** For the grill, take 75g (3oz) of the black icing and roll out until large enough to cut out four 28 x 1cm (11 x ½in) strips. Wrap one strip around the cake so the lower edge of the strip is 4cm (1½in) lower than the bottom edge of the brown icing, pressing gently into the buttercream to secure. Cut off any excess icing at the back. Position the three remaining strips in the same way, overlapping the strips slightly so the final strip meets the brown icing.

**7** Reserve 100g (3½oz) of the brown icing. For the skirt, roll out the remainder to a 50 x 15cm (20 x 6in) rectangle. Neaten one long side with a knife and wrap the icing around the cake so the neatened edge meets the grill. Smooth the icing down, overlapping it slightly at the back and securing the overlap in place with a damp paintbrush. Trim off the excess around the base. Use the trimmings to patch up any gaps in the icing at the back of the cake. Lightly spray the skirt area with more gold spray. As you do this, hold a piece of card or paper against the grill so you don't get any on the black icing. Carefully transfer the cake to the cake board (this is easiest done by lowering it gently in place with a fish slice). Roll out the remaining black icing until large enough to cut out a 45 x 2cm (18 x ¾in) strip. Secure around the base of the Dalek for the bumper. Reserve the trimmings.

**8** Roll out half the reserved brown icing until large enough to cut out two 30 x 1cm (12 x ½in) strips. Secure around the 'waist' of the cake, leaving a small gap in between the strips.

**9** Mark vertical panels around the icing skirt using the back of a knife. Shape small balls of the reserved brown icing, about the size of a pea, and flatten. Position four pieces in each of the panels. Use silver food colouring and a fine paintbrush to paint the brown strips around the middle of the cake and all the small round decorations.

**10** For the eye stalk, push one candy stick into the dome so 2.5cm (1in) is visible. Decorate with black icing, pushing a ball of icing onto the end and adding an even smaller ball of yellow icing to the end. Push a small 'plunger'-shaped piece of black icing onto the end of another candy stick and push into the cake until sufficiently supported. Wrap a flat piece of white icing around the remaining candy stick to shape the gun stick. Push slightly further into the cake. Paint the gun with silver food colouring. Shape two small lights in white icing and secure to the top of the dome.

# DALEKTABLE ARMY

Daleks don't eat – or at least, not in the way that we do. But if they did, they'd certainly enjoy these delicious cupcakes. Silver cupcake cases, candy sticks and sweets make an easy and effective decoration for these Dalek teatime cakes. Both the sponge and topping are flavoured with coconut, but you can easily substitute another flavouring like vanilla, orange or lemon instead.

## MAKES 10 CAKES

150g (5oz) slightly salted butter, softened
150g (5oz) caster sugar
3 medium eggs
175g (6oz) self-raising flour
50g (2oz) creamed coconut

### TO DECORATE:

200g (7oz) slightly salted butter, softened
300g (11oz) icing sugar
1½ tsp coconut extract
black food colouring
blue mini candy-covered chocolates
10 small black gummy sweets
10 candy sticks
small bit of white ready-to-roll icing
tube of black writing icing

### YOU WILL NEED:

a 12-hole cupcake tray and a 12-hole mini cupcake tray with foil cupcake cases

**1** Preheat the oven to 180°C/350°F/gas 4. Line 10 sections of a 12-hole cupcake tray with foil cupcake cases. Fit 10 foil mini cupcake cases into a mini cupcake tray (if you don't have a mini cupcake tray, use double layer cases and arrange on a baking sheet; the extra layer will stop the cases collapsing as they bake). Put the butter, caster sugar, eggs and flour in a bowl. If the coconut is very solid, grate it into the bowl. If slightly softened, it's easier to finely chop it and add. Beat the ingredients together for a couple of minutes until pale and creamy.

**2** Divide among the paper cases, filling them no more than two-thirds full. Bake the larger cupcakes for 17–20 minutes and the smaller ones for 12 minutes. The cakes should be risen and just firm to the touch. Transfer to a wire rack to cool completely.

**3** For the buttercream, beat together the butter, icing sugar and coconut extract until pale and creamy. Beat in a little black food colouring until it is pale grey.

**4** Pile the buttercream on top of the large cupcakes. Smooth out with a palette knife to a deep, dome shape. Invert a small cupcake on top and smooth the buttercream out to fill any gaps between the cakes.

**5** Press vertical rows of the blue sweets around the cakes. Push a small black sweet onto one end of each candy stick and press into the cakes, just under the small cupcake cases. Roll pea-sized balls of white icing and flatten slightly. Secure to the small cupcake cases with a dot of black writing icing for the eye stalks. Pipe further dots of black icing over the white.

**COOK'S TIPS**

If the black sweets are very hard you can soften them in the microwave. Do this very briefly and one at a time in short spurts. Take care as they will quickly overheat. If you can't get hold of small sweets, shape black ready-to-roll icing instead.

"SEEK LOCATE TERMINATE"

# SWEET SILENCE

Luckily this cake isn't like the real Silence. So if you get distracted while making it and look away, you won't immediately forget what you were doing. The success of the cake relies largely on getting a good sponge shape before you cover it with icing. Bake the cake in an ovenproof mixing bowl so you start with a domed cake, ready for cutting into shape. Allow plenty of time for the decoration. This is a creation you'll get thoroughly absorbed in – and love the results!

## SERVES 12

300g (11oz) slightly salted butter, softened
300g (11oz) caster sugar
1 tbsp vanilla extract
5 medium eggs, beaten
375g (13oz) self-raising flour

**TO FINISH:**

150g (5oz) slightly salted butter
200g (7oz) icing sugar, plus extra for dusting
6–8 tbsp strawberry or raspberry jam
900g (2lb) flesh-coloured ready-to-roll icing (see Cook's tips on poge 78)
burgundy food colouring powder
small bit of red ready-to-roll icing
black food colouring

**YOU WILL NEED:**

a large 3.4 litre (6 pint) mixing bowl, a fine paintbrush and a pastry brush

**1** Preheat the oven to 160°C/325°F/gas 3. Grease a large mixing bowl with a capacity of 3.4 litres (6 pints). Line the base with a large circle of baking parchment. Beat the butter, caster sugar and vanilla extract in a bowl until pale and creamy. Gradually beat in the eggs, a little at a time. If the mixture starts to separate, beat in a spoonful of the flour.

**2** Sift the flour into the bowl and fold in gently until combined. Turn into the prepared bowl and level the surface. Bake for about 1¼–1½ hours or until the surface is just firm to the touch. A skewer inserted into the centre should come out clean. Leave to cool completely in the bowl.

**3** Loosen the edges of the cake and invert out of the bowl. If the cake surface has risen in the centre during baking, you'll need to slice this off so the cake sits flat on the surface with the rounded side face up.

**4** To shape the face, you're aiming to create a sort of pear shape. First cut two slices off the sides of the cake, keeping the knife vertical but angling the cuts so the cake is narrower at the 'chin'. The Silence has a bony area around the centre of the face, so keep the hard edge of the cut for the central third of the face and round off the edge over the top third for the skull and the bottom third for the chin. (All the pieces of cake you've cut away will freeze well for a trifle another time).

CONTINUES ON NEXT PAGE ▶

**5** Beat together the butter and icing sugar until pale and creamy. Cut the cake horizontally into three layers. Sandwich back together with the jam and half the buttercream. Spread the remaining buttercream over the top and sides.

**6** To shape the face, use the diagram on page 152 to help you. First take a 40g (1½oz) ball of the flesh-coloured ready-to-roll icing and push it onto the thin end of the cake to elongate the chin. Shape two 40g (1½oz) balls of icing into sausage shapes, tapered at one end, to form the eye sockets. Shape two 10g (¼oz) balls of icing to a point, and place above the sockets to form the upper eye ridges. Finally, shape two 10g (¼oz) balls of icing into rectangles to form the cheekbones. Position all these pieces on the cake as shown in the diagram.

**7** Roll out the remaining icing on a surface dusted with icing sugar to an oval shape, 5mm (¼in) thick. Lift over the cake and let the icing fall down the sides. Ease it to fit around the sides of the cake and trim off the excess around the base. Keep the trimmings in case you need any for patching up. Transfer the cake to a board for serving (see Cook's tips).

## COOK'S TIPS

You can buy flesh-coloured ready-to-roll icing from cake decorating suppliers. Alternatively, knead a very small amount of red and brown paste food colouring into white icing.

Use any board or flat plate for serving. We've used a framed chalkboard and drawn a jacket, shirt and tie to finish. If you do this, first transfer the cake to a piece of baking parchment on a chopping board. Cut around the base of the cake (a scalpel is ideal for this) so the paper doesn't show. Then transfer to the chalkboard.

**8** While the icing is still soft and pliable, mould it around the eyes and lower face. Ease the icing carefully into the eye sockets so you don't tear it (though if you do, you can patch it up). Use the handle tip of a paintbrush to press the nose shape into the icing and to add further lines, cracks and crannies.

**9** Use a dry pastry brush to brush the burgundy food colouring powder into the eye areas and lightly over other areas of the cake to accentuate the bony shape. (Practise on a little leftover icing first.) Use a fine paintbrush to paint the grooves and nose.

**10** Take two pea-sized balls of red icing and flatten into oval shapes for the eyes. Position right at the top of the eye sockets. Paint the centres black, leaving a fine red rim.

# SALLY SPARROW'S WEEPING ANGEL CAKE

The first encounter that Sally Sparrow had with a Weeping Angel was in a spooky old house where she found a warning message from the Doctor hidden under the wallpaper. Sadly, it wasn't edible wallpaper, but the message was still effective. The idea behind this creation has to be an angel cake even if the Weeping Angel is far from angelic! The cake is layered up with cream cheese frosting and decorated with ready-to-roll icing – another opportunity to show off your creative skills. The cake base can be made a few days in advance and freezes well. Once layered up with cream cheese frosting and decorated, it should be stored in a cool place and served within 2 days.

## SERVES 12

8 medium egg whites
1 tsp cream of tartar
finely grated zest of 2 lemons
¼ tsp salt
200g (7oz) caster sugar
90g (3¼oz) plain flour

**FOR THE FROSTING:**
400g (14oz) full-fat cream cheese
125g (4¼oz) icing sugar
1 tsp lemon juice
50g (2oz) butter, very soft

**TO DECORATE:**
500g (1lb 2oz) white ready-to-roll icing
green, brown and black paste food colourings
5 tbsp icing sugar, plus extra for dusting

**YOU WILL NEED:**
a 33 x 22cm (13 x 8½in) Swiss roll tin or similar-sized shallow tin, a paintbrush and a paper piping bag or polythene food bag

**1** Preheat the oven to 160°C/325°F/gas 3. Grease a 33 x 22cm (13 x 8½in) Swiss roll tin or similar-sized shallow tin and line with baking parchment. Put the egg whites in a large, thoroughly clean bowl and whisk until frothy. Add the cream of tartar, lemon zest and salt and whisk until the egg whites are softly peaking. Sprinkle in a heaped dessertspoonful of the caster sugar and whisk briefly to mix. Continue to add the caster sugar, a heaped spoonful at a time, whisking well after each addition.

**2** Sift the flour onto a piece of kitchen paper. Sift again, this time into the bowl. Fold in with a large metal spoon until combined. Spoon half the mixture into the tin and spread level. Bake for 15 minutes until just firm to the touch. Carefully slide the cake and paper out of the tin. Re-line the tin and bake the remaining mixture in the same way. Leave to cool.

**CONTINUES ON NEXT PAGE** ▶

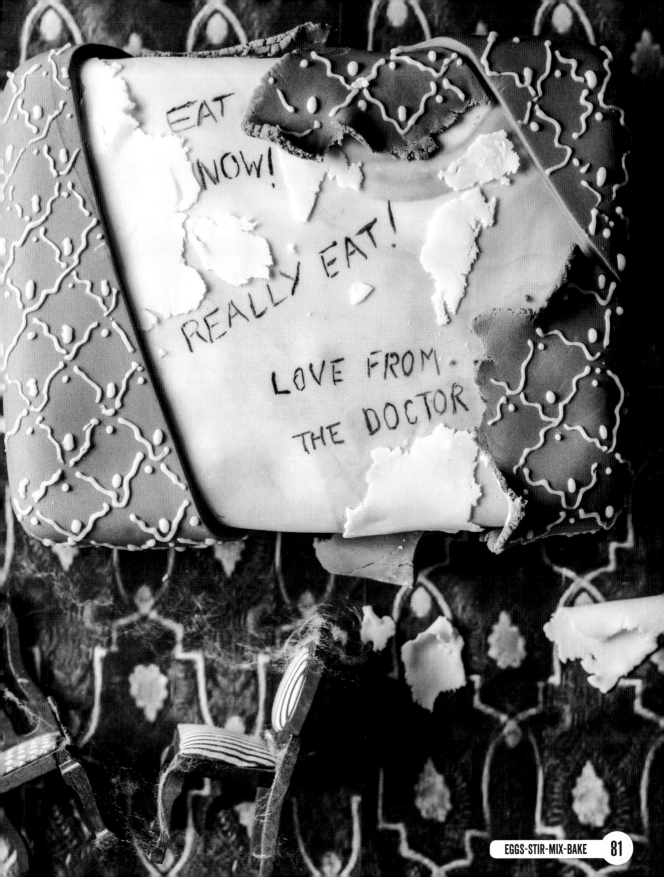

**3** For the frosting, beat the cream cheese in a bowl until softened. Add the icing sugar, lemon juice and butter and beat until completely smooth. Cut each of the cakes in half widthways and place one layer on a serving board. Reserve a third of the frosting and use the remainder to sandwich the cake layers together on the board. Position the top layer of cake so the flat base is uppermost. Spread the remaining frosting over the top and sides.

**4** Take 200g (7oz) of the ready-to-roll icing and knead on the work surface to soften slightly. Knead in a dash of green food colouring, a dash of brown and a dash of black until the icing is streaked with colour. Thinly roll out on a surface dusted with icing sugar and cut out a rectangle that's large enough to cover the top and long sides of the cake. Lift over the cake, smooth out gently and trim off any excess.

**5** For the peeling wallpaper, take a 15g (½oz) piece of white icing and roll out as thinly as you can. Tear off small pieces and secure to the top and bottom of the cake with a dampened paintbrush to resemble raggedy patches of peeled paper. Add a couple of pieces to the board too.

**6** For the wallpaper, knead more green and black colouring into the remaining white icing until a deep, dark green. Thinly roll out half the icing and lay diagonally over the left hand side of the cake as in the photograph. Fit the icing down the sides and trim off the excess around the base. Roll out the remaining icing and secure diagonally on the other side of the cake, fitting the icing down the sides. Use the icing trimmings to add further sections of wallpaper, keeping the edges raggedy as though peeled away from the base. Crumple up more trimmings and scatter onto the board.

**7** Put the icing sugar in a bowl and stir in a few drops of water to make a thin paste. Transfer to a paper piping bag or one corner of a polythene food bag and snip off the merest tip. Use to pipe the wallpaper design.

**8** Dilute a little black paste food colouring with water so it has the consistency of thick paint. Using a fine paintbrush, paint the words onto the icing as shown in the photograph.

# "DON'T BLINK

## Don't even blink.
## Blink and you're
# DEAD."

# TIME AND RELATIVE DIMENSIONS IN CAKE

Wherever and whenever he ends up, the Doctor almost certainly got there in the TARDIS. It can travel anywhere in time and space. But wherever he ends up, you can be sure he'll soon be in trouble… This birthday cake depicts the TARDIS tumbling through space on Doctor Who's latest time travelling mission. A moist and fruity carrot cake on the inside, it's a vision of sparkling space dust on the outside. Carrot cake keeps well once iced, so you can make it several days ahead of the party.

## SERVES 12–15

250g (9oz) carrots
225g (8oz) slightly salted butter, softened
250g (9oz) light muscovado sugar
2 tsp vanilla extract
4 medium eggs, beaten
325g (11½oz) self-raising flour
2 tsp baking powder
2 tsp ground mixed spice
125g (4¼oz) ground almonds
125g (4¼oz) sultanas

**TO DECORATE:**
150g (5oz) slightly salted butter, softened
200g (7oz) icing sugar, plus extra for dusting
400g (14oz) dark blue ready-to-roll icing
25g (1oz) orange ready-to-roll icing
250g (9oz) white ready-to-roll icing
1 mini marshmallow
250g (9oz) black ready-to-roll icing
edible gold and silver glitter

**YOU WILL NEED:**
a large 3.4 litre (6 pint) mixing bowl, an empty 400g (14oz) or 200g (7oz) food tin (such as for condensed milk or tinned tomatoes), a paintbrush and a paper piping bag fitted with a writing nozzle

CONTINUES ON NEXT PAGE

"It's a telephone box from the 1950s. **IT'S A DISGUISE.**"

**1** Preheat the oven to 160°C/325°F/gas 3. Grease a large mixing bowl with a capacity of 3.4 litres (6 pints). Remove both ends from an empty food tin. Wash, then grease and line the base and sides with baking parchment. Place the tin on a small baking sheet lined with baking parchment. Line the base of the bowl with a large circle of baking parchment.

**2** Finely grate the carrots. Beat the butter, muscavado sugar and vanilla extract in a bowl until pale and creamy. Gradually beat in the eggs, a little at a time. If the mixture starts to separate, beat in a spoonful of the flour.

**3** Add the flour, baking powder, mixed spice and ground almonds and stir gently to combine. Stir in the sultanas and carrots. Spoon 150g (5oz) of the cake mixture into the food tin. Spoon the remainder into the large bowl and level both surfaces. Bake the cake in the tin for 30 minutes and the cake in the bowl for 1¼–1½ hours or until firm to the touch and a skewer inserted into the centre comes out clean. Leave to cool completely in the tin and bowl.

**4** Loosen the edges of the large cake and invert onto a large round plate or board. Remove the cake from the tin and peel away the paper. Cut off four sides so you end up with a tall square block for the TARDIS. Beat together the butter and icing sugar until smooth and creamy. Spread a thin layer over the sides and top of the TARDIS and a thicker layer over the domed cake, making sure you fill the gap around the base of the cake.

**5** Thinly roll out 150g (5oz) of the dark blue icing on a surface lightly dusted with icing sugar. Cut out four rectangles, one for each side of the TARDIS. Secure in place, pressing gently into the buttercream. Re-roll the trimmings and cut out a square, slightly larger than the base of the TARDIS. Place on a square of baking parchment and spread a little buttercream in the centre. Position the TARDIS on top. Cut another square of icing, the same size as the base, and secure to the top of the TARDIS. Re-roll the trimmings and cut out a slightly smaller square. Position this on top of the roof, securing with a dampened paintbrush.

**6** Roll out a little orange icing as thinly as you can for the TARDIS windows. Cut small squares and secure in place. Add a smaller square of the white icing for the noticeboard. Secure a mini marshmallow to the roof, again with a dampened paintbrush. Put the reserved buttercream in a paper piping bag fitted with a writing nozzle and use to pipe decorative lines over the TARDIS.

**7** Roll out the black icing and the remaining white and blue icings under the palms of your hands, each into a long thick sausage. Squeeze the three colours together and roll again into a longer sausage shape. Fold and scrunch the icing together and re-roll. Keep doing this for several more rolls until the colours start to marble and merge together. Roll out the icing with a rolling pin to a round large enough to cover the domed cake. Lift into position and smooth around the sides, trimming off the excess around the base.

**8** Sprinkle the gold and silver glitter in trailing lines over the cake. If it doesn't stick, very lightly dampen the area you want to sprinkle over with a paintbrush first. Lightly brush the base of the TARDIS with water and secure to the top of the cake, slightly to one side of centre. If you feel the TARDIS is a bit unbalanced, use a piece of bamboo skewer or cake pop stick to hold it in place.

# CHRISTMAS SNOWMAN

Snowmen are usually happy, jolly-looking figures. But not the ones created by the Great Intelligence. They were really quite vicious, and didn't enter into the Christmas spirit at all. For Doctor Who fans looking for an alternative Christmas cake, this could be the answer – the snowman with the scary smile! It's a traditional rich fruit cake, finished with marzipan and royal icing so you can make it well in advance – job done!

## SERVES 16–20

200g (7oz) slightly salted butter, softened
200g (7oz) dark muscovado sugar
2 tsp ground mixed spice
2 tsp ground ginger
finely grated zest and squeezed juice of 1 orange
3 medium eggs, beaten
250g (9oz) plain flour
850g (1lb 14oz) mixed dried fruit
100g (3½oz) natural glacé cherries, chopped
50g (2oz) blanched almonds, chopped

### TO DECORATE:

3 tbsp apricot jam
black paste food colouring
1kg (2¼lb) white marzipan
400–450g (14oz–1lb) icing sugar, plus extra for dusting
2 medium egg whites
desiccated coconut, to sprinkle

### YOU WILL NEED:

a 2.25 litre (4 pint) and a 1.2 litre (2 pint) ovenproof mixing bowl

**1** Preheat the oven to 140°C/275°F/gas 1. Grease a 2.25 litre (4 pint) and a 1.2 litre (2 pint) ovenproof mixing bowl and line the bases with circles of baking parchment. Put the butter, muscovado sugar, spices and orange zest in a large bowl and beat with a hand-held electric whisk until smooth and creamy. Gradually beat in the eggs, a little at a time, adding a spoonful of the flour if the mixture starts to separate. Stir in the orange juice. Fold in the flour, then the dried fruit, glacé cherries and almonds.

**2** Spoon 1.2kg (2½lb) of the mixture into the smaller bowl and level the surface. Spoon the remainder into the larger bowl. Bake the larger (but shallower) bowl for 1½ hours (as the bowl is shallower, the cake will cook faster) and the smaller bowl for 3 hours. The cakes are cooked when the surface feels firm and a skewer inserted into the centre comes out clean. Leave to cool completely in the bowl.

**3** Loosen the edges of the cakes with a knife and ease them out of the bowls. Invert the larger, shallow cake onto a serving plate or board. Using a sharp knife, round off the edges of the cake baked in the smaller bowl so it's reasonably round. Position on top of the other cake.

**4** Melt the jam in a small pan with 1 tablespoon water until softened. Press through a sieve and brush all over the surface of the cake.

CONTINUES ON NEXT PAGE ▶

**5** Knead the black food colouring into 50g (2oz) of the marzipan. Trace the mouth and eye templates (page 150) onto paper and cut out. Roll out the remaining marzipan on a surface dusted with icing sugar to a 33cm (13in) round. Lift over the cake and fit around the sides. Push the marzipan into the neck, moulding it to fit. This needn't be neat as it'll be covered with icing. Trim off the excess around the base. Shape the trimmings into a ball and flatten out under the palms of your hands. Place on top of the head and smooth out. Thinly roll out the black marzipan and cut around the eye and mouth templates. Secure onto one side of the head. If the marzipan doesn't stay in place, dampen the back with water.

**6** Beat the egg whites in a bowl with 400g (14oz) of the icing sugar until completely smooth. The icing should form soft peaks. If the consistency is soft and losing its shape, beat in a little more icing sugar. Spread a thick layer over the marzipan just above the mouth. Using the tip of a palette knife, pull the icing down at intervals over the mouth to resemble teeth. Spread the remaining icing around the rest of the mouth and the eyes, then over the rest of the cake. Smooth the icing down with a palette knife. Sprinkle coconut over the cake and board, and pat down lightly.

"Do you feel it?
WINTER IS
COMING."

# PEEK-A-BOO PANDORICA

If the Doctor was surprised at what was inside the Pandorica when it opened, then your guests will be too. Though it won't be the Doctor himself – or even Amy Pond – inside, this impressively-sized cube-shaped cake would make a brilliant birthday cake for a Doctor Who fan of any age. Like the Pandorica itself, the cake is full of surprises when cut into as a feast of sweet treats spill out. The real Pandorica lasted for over 2,000 years, but ideally make the two cake bases and the sides for the box just 3 days before serving. You can then assemble and decorate the cake the day before.

## SERVES 16–20

**FOR THE CAKE:**

150g (5oz) cocoa powder
250ml (9fl oz) boiling water
350g (12oz) plain chocolate, chopped
300g (11oz) slightly salted butter, softened
600g (1lb 5oz) light muscovado sugar
6 medium eggs
550g (1¼lb) plain flour
2 tsp bicarbonate of soda

**FOR THE BUTTERCREAM:**

175g (6oz) unsalted butter, softened
250g (9oz) icing sugar
25g (1oz) cocoa powder

**TO DECORATE:**

1.75kg (4lb) dark grey ready-to-roll icing (see Cook's tips on page 94)
icing sugar, for dusting
about 250g (9oz) chocolates and sugar-coated sweets, preferably green and blue
black food spray (optional)

**YOU WILL NEED:**

a 15cm (6in) square cake tin, an 11cm (4½in) cutter, 25cm (10in), 23cm (9in) and 20cm (8in) square silver cake boards and a 1.5cm (⅝ in) wide grey ribbon

**1** Preheat the oven to 160°C/325°F/gas 3. Line a 15cm (6in) square cake tin with a double thickness of greaseproof paper. Grease the paper.

**2** Put 75g (3oz) of the cocoa powder in a heatproof bowl. Pour the boiling water over the cocoa powder, whisking well until combined. Immediately tip in 175g (6oz) of the chopped chocolate and leave until the chocolate has melted, stirring occasionally.

**3** Put 150g (5oz) of the butter, 300g (11oz) of the muscovado sugar, 3 eggs, 275g (10oz) of the flour and 1 teaspoon bicarbonate of soda in a large bowl and beat with a hand-held electric whisk until smooth and creamy. Stir in the chocolate mixture until combined. Turn into the tin and level the surface. Bake for 1½–1¾ hours or until the cake feels firm to the touch and a skewer inserted into the centre comes out clean. Leave to cool in the tin, then turn out onto a wire rack. Bake another chocolate cake using the remaining cake ingredients.

**4** For the side panel decoration, line a baking sheet or board with baking parchment. Take a small piece of grey icing to practise the indentations as follows. It's best to lightly knead ready-to-roll icing first to make it more pliable. Collect three or four objects that have a small square or rectangular-shaped end. Metal cutlery, wooden chopsticks, giant matchsticks and even the end of a small pencil sharpener are ideal. Try pressing a line of these into the icing you've rolled to see if the shapes are convincing for the Pandorica.

**5** Roll out 200g (7oz) of the grey icing on a surface dusted with icing sugar. Keep the icing as square as possible in shape and roll out until you're able to cut out a neat 15cm (6in) square (see Cook's tips on page 94). It's easier if you transfer the icing to the baking parchment before cutting so it holds its shape. Gently impress an 11cm (4½in) plain round cutter into the icing to mark, but not cut through, a circle. Gently press the items you've collected into the marked circle. Mark a 9cm (3½in) circle

CONTINUES ON NEXT PAGE ▶

inside the first and make indentations around this, followed by a 6cm (2½in) circle in the centre. Decorate in the same way. Mark one more circle in the centre, about 4cm (1½in). Make three more panels in the same way.

**6** Thinly roll out 250g (9oz) of the grey icing on a surface dusted with icing sugar until large enough to cover the 25cm (10in) cake board. Lightly dampen the board and lift the rolled icing over it. Smooth out to the edges and trim off the excess with a sharp knife. Cover the 23cm (9in) board with 200g (7oz) icing and the 20cm (8in) board with 150g (5oz) icing. Leave the boards and side panels to harden for 2 days.

**7** For the buttercream, beat together the butter, icing sugar and cocoa powder until smooth and creamy. If the cakes have domed up in the centre during baking, cut a slice off so the tops are level. To make sure the cake will be a cube shape when assembled, measure the height and width, which must be the same. If necessary, trim a little more off each cake. Cut each cake in half horizontally. Cut the centres out of two of the layers to leave a wall of cake 3cm (1¼in) thick around the edges.

**8** Spread the edges of one of the solid cake layers with a little buttercream and place a hollowed-out cake layer on top. Spread the edges of this with buttercream and position the other hollowed-out cake on top. Spread the edges of this with more buttercream. Fill the cake cavity with the chocolates and sweets and position the remaining cake layer on top. Place the iced cake boards on top of one another to create steps. Transfer the cake to the top board.

**9** Spread a thin layer of buttercream over the sides of the cake with a palette knife. Gently lift one panel on one hand, invert it onto the other and peel away the paper. Press the panel gently against one side of the cake so the panel sits squarely at one end with the cake, but juts out 5mm (¼in) at the other. Position the next panel against this and then the third and fourth.

**10** Spread more buttercream over the top of the cake until level with the top of the iced sides. Roll out the remaining grey icing and cut out a square to fit the top of the cake. Dampen the top edges of the side panels with water and position the top, smoothing down gently to fit. Secure a grey ribbon around the sides of the boards with double-sided tape or dressmaker's pins. If liked, spray a little black spray around the edges of the box to create an aged effect.

## COOK'S TIPS

Ready-coloured icing is the easiest to use and is available online and from cake decorating shops. Alternatively, you can buy white ready-to-roll icing and knead in black food colouring until the icing is dark grey. To make a professional-looking cake, you'll need perfectly measured side panels so they meet neatly at the corners. Before rolling out the side panels, measure the width of the cake. The panels should be cut to this width plus an additional 5mm (¼in).

# FRUIT SALAD EYE STALKS

In some parts of the galaxy, people fighting the Daleks collect the eye stalks of Daleks they've destroyed as trophies. But these Dalek eye stalks are a lot easier and less dangerous to get hold of. A few apple slices, pieces of kiwi fruit and a plum threaded onto skewers make incredibly effective-looking Dalek eye stalks! Use metal kebab skewers if you have them as they're sturdier. If not, bamboo skewers will do. Serve with a bowl of honey yoghurt for a fun, easy pud.

## MAKES 4 KEBABS

3–4 small red-skinned
    eating apples
2 tsp lemon or lime juice
4 round plums
4 kiwi fruit
4 blueberries
3 tbsp clear honey
100g (3½oz) Greek-style yoghurt

**YOU WILL NEED:**
4 skewers

**1** Cut the apples into thin slices, leaving the cores intact. Brush each side of the apple slices with lemon or lime juice to stop them browning.

**2** Cut a thin slice off the stalk end of each plum. Use the tip of a sharp knife or an apple corer to ease out the stones, keeping the fruit intact.

**3** Peel the kiwi fruit and use an apple corer to cut out as many lengths of kiwi as you can from each. Cut four of the lengths into smaller 1cm (½in) lengths.

**4** Carefully thread a length of kiwi onto a skewer. Add an apple slice, then a short length of kiwi. Add three more apple slices, threading a short length of kiwi between each. Thread another long length of kiwi fruit. Push a 2cm (¾in) length of kiwi into a plum to fill the cavity. Thread the plum onto the skewer so the cut side is threaded last. You'll need a 5mm (¼in) tip of the skewer left at the end after threading the fruit, so if necessary slide the fruits back towards the tip. Push a blueberry onto the tip. Make the remaining kebabs in the same way.

**5** For the honey yoghurt dip, beat the honey into the Greek-style yoghurt. Serve in a bowl with the fruit kebabs.

# EXTERMINATED JELLY SKELETON

If you get shot by a Dalek – and I wouldn't recommend it – then the blast from its gun is so powerful that your whole skeleton becomes visible. These piped meringues create incredibly effective 'bones', making a fun dessert for a kids' party or family gathering. The meringues can be made several days in advance and stored in an airtight container. The jelly's best made up to a day ahead.

## SERVES 6

2 medium egg whites
100g (3½oz) caster sugar
3 eating apples
2 tsp lemon juice
2 tablets lime-flavoured jelly
400ml (14fl oz) boiling water
lightly whipped cream, to serve

**YOU WILL NEED:**
a large piping bag fitted with a
1cm (½in) plain piping nozzle

**1** Preheat the oven to 120°C/250°F/gas ½. Line two baking sheets with baking parchment.

**2** Put the egg whites in a thoroughly clean bowl and whisk with a hand-held electric whisk until softly peaking. Sprinkle in a heaped tablespoonful of the sugar and whisk for 15 seconds. Continue to whisk the mixture, adding a spoonful of sugar at a time and whisking well between each addition, until the meringue is stiff and glossy.

**3** Spoon into a large piping bag fitted with a 1cm (½in) plain piping nozzle. Pipe an 8–9cm (3–3½in) length of meringue onto the paper. Pipe an extra blob at each end to create a bone shape. Carry on until you have used up all the mixture. Bake for about 1 hour or until the meringues feel crisp and dry. Leave to cool completely on the paper.

**4** For the jelly, peel, core and finely grate the apples into a bowl and stir in the lemon juice. Separate the jelly cubes into a bowl. Add the boiling water and stir frequently until the jelly has dissolved. Pour over the grated apple, stir in 300ml (½ pint) cold water and leave until cool but not set. Transfer to a shallow serving dish and chill for several hours until set.

**5** To serve, arrange some of the meringue bones on top of the jelly. Serve with whipped cream.

# ADIPOSE PAVLOVA

The Adipose were made of people's excess body fat. But unlike the little white aliens in Doctor Who, this dessert 'Adipose' is big, chubby and completely fat-free! It's a crisp meringue on the outside with a fruity little heart. Serve with lightly whipped cream for a delicious pavlova-style pud.

## SERVES 6

4 medium egg whites
125g (4¼oz) caster sugar
75g (3oz) golden caster sugar
2 tsp vanilla extract
150g (5oz) mixed raspberries,
   blackberries and blueberries
1 mini marshmallow
lightly whipped cream, to serve

**COOK'S TIP**

If you think the meringue might break up as you transfer it to a platter or board, cut off the surplus paper by cutting around the meringue with a scalpel, then slide onto the platter or board.

**1** Preheat the oven to 140°C/275°F/gas 1. Using the photograph as a guide, draw a large rectangle measuring 21 x 18cm (8½ x 7in) onto a sheet of baking parchment. Round off the corners with the pencil to create the Adipose body shape. Add chubby hands halfway down the sides of the body and equally chubby feet, if liked. (The paper will be turned over before spreading with meringue, so if you want to position one hand as though waving, do this on the right hand side of the body.) Turn the parchment over and place on a baking sheet.

**2** Whisk the egg whites in a thoroughly clean bowl until softly peaking. Combine the two sugars, add 1 tablespoon to the whites and whisk for 15 seconds. Continue adding the sugar, a spoonful at a time and whisking well between each addition. Whisk in the vanilla extract with the last of the sugar.

**3** Secure the parchment paper to the baking sheet by placing a blob of meringue under each corner of the paper. Spoon half the meringue into the figure and spread to the edges with a palette knife. Spread more meringue into the hand and feet areas. Reserve three of the largest blueberries. Scatter the remaining fruits into the centre of the meringue and spoon the rest of the meringue on top. Spread to cover the fruits.

**4** Using a palette knife, spread all the meringue as smoothly as you can. Make slight dips into the meringue with the back of a teaspoon where the eyes will be positioned.

**5** Bake for 1½ hours or until the surface feels crisp to the touch. Leave to cool completely on the baking sheet. Loosen the meringue from the paper with a fish slice (see Cook's tip) and carefully transfer the meringue to a large flat serving platter or board. Position two reserved blueberries for eyes. Halve the remaining blueberry and cut a slightly smiling mouth from one half. Position on the meringue and add the mini marshmallow for the single tooth. Serve with whipped cream.

HELLO, SWEETIES

# DAVROS' THIRD EYE BROWNIES

Almost everything about Davros, the creator of the Daleks, has been augmented or enhanced to keep him alive. That includes his vision. His own eyes barely work any more, so he has an electronic eye in the middle of his forehead. Scooped semicircles of fresh pear make effective, glassy-looking eyes, particularly when they're brushed with blue-coloured honey! Do this just before serving for maximum impact.

## MAKES 12 BROWNIES

200g (7oz) plain chocolate, chopped
125g (4¼oz) slightly salted butter
2 medium eggs
175g (6oz) light muscovado sugar
1 tsp vanilla extract
75g (3oz) self-raising flour

### TO FINISH:

2–3 large ripe pears, peeled and cored
1 tbsp lemon juice
75g (3oz) milk chocolate, chopped
150g (5oz) slightly salted butter
150g (5oz) icing sugar
3 tbsp cocoa powder
1 tbsp clear honey
a few drops of blue food colouring

### YOU WILL NEED:

a 12-hole muffin tray and a piping bag fitted with a 1cm (½in) star nozzle

1 Preheat the oven to 180°C/350°F/gas 4. Grease a 12-hole muffin tray. Put half the plain chocolate in a heatproof bowl with the butter and melt, either in short spurts in the microwave or by resting the bowl over a pan of gently simmering water. Stir occasionally until completely smooth.

2 Put the eggs, muscovado sugar and vanilla extract in a bowl and whisk with a hand-held electric whisk for 2–3 minutes until thickened and pale. Stir in the melted chocolate mixture. Sift the flour into the bowl, add the remaining chopped chocolate and gently stir the ingredients together. Spoon into the muffin tray holes.

3 Bake for 17–20 minutes until slightly risen and a crust has formed. The cakes will still feel slightly soft. Leave to cool completely in the tray. Loosen the edges with a knife and lift out.

4 To shape the eyes, use a 1 tablespoon (15ml/½fl oz) measuring spoon and scoop semicircles of flesh out of the pears. Place in a bowl and coat in the lemon juice to prevent browning. (Dice the remaining fruit, toss with a little extra lemon juice and reserve for a fruit salad.) Melt the milk chocolate as above. Beat the butter and icing sugar in a bowl until creamy and stir in the melted chocolate and cocoa powder. Place in a piping bag fitted with a 1cm (½in) star nozzle. Pipe a blob onto the centre of each cake. Place a piece of pear on top and pipe some chocolate cream on either side.

5 Just before serving, mix together the honey and blue food colouring and brush over the pear eyes.

"I regret I cannot **OPEN MY EYES.**"

# TIME ROTOR SODAS

The central column of the TARDIS control console is sometimes referred to as the Time Rotor, although the term has also been used for other controls. But it's the transparent central column that we're recreating here in edible form. The 'glasses' for this fun drink are, in fact, made of coloured ice. All you need to make them are two disposable plastic drinks tumblers, a drop of food colouring and a bit of freezer space! Allow plenty of freezing time, at least overnight, so you can freeze the ice, remove from the plastic and re-freeze the ice glasses, all ready for filling with a lovely minty ice cream soda.

## FOR EACH SODA

a little green or blue food colouring
2–3 scoops of mint, vanilla or
    pistachio ice cream
chilled lemonade or cream soda

**YOU WILL NEED:**
inexpensive clear disposable tumblers are the best for making ice glasses. You can make any size 'glass' as long as the inner tumbler is about half the capacity of the larger one. So if you have a 500ml (18fl oz) capacity tumbler for the larger size, the smaller one should be about 250ml (9fl oz)

**1** First choose suitable disposable tumblers (see left). Pour cold water into the larger glass until it is about two-thirds full. Add a few drops of green or blue food colouring and stir to mix. Press the smaller tumbler into the centre so the water level rises to the top between the glasses. Half fill the small tumbler with baking beans, dried beans reserved for baking blind or any other freezerproof, heavy weight such as old-fashioned kitchen weights. Secure a strip of tape from the top of the inner tumbler down the side of the larger one. Secure another strip on the other side of the tumblers. This will ensure that the smaller tumbler stays right in the centre of the larger one as it freezes. Carefully transfer to the freezer and freeze until completely solid, ideally overnight.

**2** Remove the weights from the small tumbler and peel away the tape. Fill the small tumbler with very hot but not boiling water, leave for 2–3 seconds, then tip out. Twist the small tumbler and ease out of the ice. If it refuses to budge, fill with hot water for another couple of seconds and try again, but take care not to melt the ice. If the ice shows any sign of melting, return it to the freezer for a couple of hours.

**3** Fill a large bowl or jug with hot water. Dip the large tumbler into the water right up to the rim for a couple of seconds. Lift out and twist the tumbler away from the ice. If necessary, re-dip the tumbler. Once removed, return the ice tumbler to the freezer for at least 1 hour or until ready to serve.

**4** Fill the ice tumbler with two or three scoops of ice cream. Top up with chilled lemonade or cream soda and serve.

# BANANA PARTY POPS

When he first met Captain Jack, the Ninth Doctor swapped Jack's gun for a banana. He worked the same trick later, as the Eleventh Doctor, with River Song. And the Tenth Doctor imparted to Rose the immortal advice: 'Always take a banana to a party... Bananas are good.' This fabulous ice cream takes the Doctor at his word and is made from one ingredient – bananas! Frozen bananas, whizzed up in a food processor, are transformed into a meltingly smooth ice cream.

## MAKES 4 ICE POPS

4 small bananas
coloured sugar sprinkles (optional)

**YOU WILL NEED:**
4 ice lolly moulds and 4 lolly sticks

**1** Freeze the whole bananas in their skins for 4–6 hours, or overnight.

**2** Run the bananas under the tap to soften their skins. Peel away the skins or scrape off with a knife, whichever is easiest. Cut each into about six chunks and put in a food processor. Process for 1–2 minutes until smooth and creamy, scraping down any pieces from the sides of the bowl.

**3** Spoon into four ice lolly moulds. If the mixture is still very thick, you might need to push a skewer through the mixture and stir to remove any air bubbles. Push lolly sticks into the mixture and freeze for at least 2 hours to firm up.

**4** Loosen from the moulds by running them under warm water. If liked, use the sugar sprinkles to decorate one side of each lolly with a Doctor Who symbol, such as a question mark. Serve and enjoy!

# FANCY A JELLY BABY?

The Doctor has always liked jelly babies. Especially the Fourth Doctor, who often offered them round, although sometimes he said it was a jelly baby when it was some other sweet. But jelly babies were certainly his preference. His favourite flavour, he once said, was orange. Homemade jelly babies taste so much fruitier and tangier than any bought ones. Strawberries and blackberries work well together both in colour and flavour, though you could use the same quantity of other soft fruits like raspberries, blackcurrants and blueberries. Once they're shaped and set, serve them as Doctor Who would, in little paper sweet bags.

## MAKES 750G (1LB 10OZ) JELLY BABIES

300g (11oz) blackberries
300g (11oz) strawberries
15 leaves gelatine
200g (7oz) caster sugar, plus extra
　sugar for coating

**YOU WILL NEED:**
a jelly baby mould

**1** Process the blackberries in a food processor or blender until puréed. Press through a sieve into a bowl. Rinse out the processor and purée the strawberries. Press through a sieve into a separate bowl.

**2** Soak the gelatine leaves in a bowl of cold water for 5 minutes. Put the sugar in a small pan with 75ml (3fl oz) cold water and heat gently until the sugar has completely dissolved. Remove from the heat and pour into a measuring jug. Lift the softened gelatine leaves out of the water and add to the syrup. Stir briefly until dissolved. Pour half the syrup into the strawberry purée, stirring well. Pour the remainder into the blackberry purée, stirring well.

**3** Carefully fill a jelly baby mould with the purées. You'll probably need to do this in batches, in which case chill the filled moulds until set and leave the remainder of the fruit purées at room temperature. If the purées start to set in the jugs, soften briefly in the microwave, or stand the jug in a pan of gently simmering water until softened.

**4** To loosen the jellies, run the back of the mould very briefly under warm water and tip the jellies out onto a piece of baking parchment. Sprinkle with extra sugar to coat. Store in a cool place (but not the fridge) until ready to serve.

# GALLIFROLLIPOPS

The TARDIS allows the Doctor and his companions to understand any language. But the Time Lords have their own language too. When written it is mainly composed of the swirling circular patterns and shapes seen on these chocolate lollipops. Check out your own designs online for Gallifreyan symbols if you're feeling ambitious, or copy the simplified ones in this recipe.

## MAKES 8 LOLLIPOPS

200g (7oz) milk chocolate, chopped
a handful each of plain, white and milk chocolate buttons, preferably in two sizes
50g (2oz) white chocolate, chopped
50g (2oz) plain chocolate, chopped

**YOU WILL NEED:**
8 wooden lolly sticks and 2 paper piping bags

**1** Line a large tray or baking sheet with baking parchment. Put the milk chocolate in a heatproof bowl and melt, either in short spurts in the microwave or by resting the bowl over a pan of gently simmering water. Stir occasionally until completely smooth. Place eight even-sized spoonfuls of the melted chocolate on the paper, spacing them well apart. Spread with the back of a spoon until 6.5cm (2½in) in diameter. Push a wooden lolly stick about halfway into each round and spread a little of the chocolate over the stick to hide it.

**2** While the chocolate is still soft, position a few of the chocolate buttons on top. You can also arrange small buttons on top of larger ones, securing the smaller ones in place with a dot of the chocolate left in the bowl. Leave in a cool place to set.

**3** Melt the white and plain chocolates in separate heatproof bowls as above. Transfer to paper piping bags. Twist the top of each bag and squeeze to see whether the chocolate flows out in a thin line. If it doesn't, snip off the merest tip. Use the chocolate to pipe decorative circles, lines and dots onto the lollies. Leave in a cool place until the chocolate has set before carefully peeling away the paper.

"It's Old High Gallifreyan, the ancient language of the **TIME LORDS.** Not many people understand it *THESE DAYS.*"

# TEA TIME LORDS

# COOKIE WHO'S WHO

The Doctor's appearance may change every time he regenerates, but that just means you can create a whole set of different Doctors to serve up to your friends and family. Prepare a batch of people-shaped cookies and assemble an assortment of coloured icing, tubes of writing icing and some melted chocolate so the family can get stuck into decorating their favourite Doctor Who figure. For the shapes, trace and cut out the template (page 149) onto paper, position on the cookie dough and cut around. Alternatively, use a gingerbread man cutter, which you can adapt by gently squeezing the limbs and bodies to slim down the shapes.

## MAKES 12 COOKIES

### FOR THE COOKIE DOUGH:
275g (10oz) plain flour, plus extra for dusting
200g (7oz) firm slightly salted butter, cut into small pieces
100g (3½oz) icing sugar
2 medium egg yolks
2 tsp vanilla extract

### TO DECORATE:
75g (3oz) plain chocolate, chopped
75g (3oz) milk chocolate, chopped
75g (3oz) white chocolate, chopped
tubes of writing icing in red, blue, yellow, white and green
50g (2oz) each of black, red, blue, white, cream, light and dark brown ready-to-roll icing
icing sugar, for dusting

### YOU WILL NEED:
a polythene food bag, 3 small paper piping bags or small polythene food bags and a fine paintbrush

**1** Put the flour in a food processor and add the butter. Process until the mixture resembles coarse breadcrumbs. Add the icing sugar, egg yolks and vanilla extract and process to a smooth dough. Wrap in a polythene food bag and chill for about 1 hour.

**2** Preheat the oven to 190°C/375°F/gas 5. Line two baking sheets with baking parchment.

**3** Roll out the dough on a lightly floured surface to a 5mm (¼in) thickness and cut out the figure shapes using the template (page 149) or a gingerbread man cutter. Space slightly apart on the baking sheets. Re-roll the trimmings to make additional shapes.

**4** Bake for 10–15 minutes until pale golden around the edges. Leave on the baking sheets for 2 minutes, then transfer to a wire rack to cool.

**5** To decorate, melt the three chocolates separately in small heatproof bowls. Do this in the microwave in short spurts or by resting the bowls, one at a time, over a small pan of gently simmering water. Pour each melted chocolate into a small paper piping bag and snip off the merest tip. You can also use small polythene food bags, spooning the chocolate into one corner, twisting the bag to push the chocolate into the corner and snipping off the smallest tip. Use the three chocolates to pipe hair onto the figures.

**6** For the Doctor Who clothes you can either pipe outlines of jackets, trousers, coats and jumpers onto the cookies using writing icing or thinly roll out small pieces of ready-to-roll icing on a surface dusted with icing sugar and cut out the shapes. For coats and jackets, you can use the cookie cutter or template as a guide, trimming the clothes to fit once you've made the basic shape with the cutter. Secure in place with a squeeze of icing from a tube. Add accessories such as hats, umbrellas, ties, bow ties and scarves, securing in place with a dampened fine paintbrush.

# KOOKIE K-9

Built by Professor Marius, who couldn't take his real dog with him into space, K-9 was a computer made of metal and plastic. But that doesn't taste nearly as nice as gingerbread! This creation takes time and a little patience, but is worth the effort – particularly if you put a little battery-powered tealight to light up his eyes. Trace the templates on page 146–8 and cut out before you start. Once assembled, K-9 will keep, loosely covered with cling film, for two days before the boiled sweets start to soften.

## SERVES 16

350g (12oz) plain flour, plus extra
    for dusting
2 tsp baking powder
2 tsp ground ginger
1 tsp ground mixed spice
100g (3½oz) firm slightly salted
    butter, cut into small pieces
150g (5oz) light muscovado sugar
3 tbsp golden syrup
1 medium egg
1 medium egg yolk
1 clear red boiled sweet

**TO FINISH:**

2 ready-made ginger loaf cakes
200g (7oz) milk chocolate, broken
    into pieces
3 marshmallows
2 pieces of dried fruit slices
25g (1oz) piece of red ready-to-roll
    icing
icing sugar, for dusting
1 clear green boiled sweet
tubes of black and green writing icing
9 small sugar-coated sweets

**YOU WILL NEED:**

a paper piping bag or small
polythene food bag and 2 x 20cm
(8in) cake pop sticks (cut down to size
with scissors if necessary)

**1** Put the flour, baking powder, ginger and mixed spice in a food processor. Add the butter and process until the mixture resembles fine breadcrumbs. Add the sugar, syrup, egg and egg yolk and process to a dough. Turn out onto a lightly floured surface and shape into a neat block. Wrap in cling film and chill for at least 30 minutes to firm up.

**2** Preheat the oven to 200°C/400°F/gas 6. Line two baking sheets with baking parchment. Roll out half the dough on a lightly floured surface to a 3mm (1/8in) thickness. Transfer to a baking sheet. Place one of the largest templates over the dough and cut around with a knife. Cut out as many more templates as you can fit over the rest of the rolled dough. Lift away the excess dough and reserve. If any of the cut out pieces are very close to each other, separate them slightly, but make sure you don't distort the shapes. Roll out the remaining dough and cut out more shapes, remembering that you'll need two of some of the shapes as indicated on the templates. Re-roll the trimmings if necessary until you've cut them all out. Using a skewer, make two large holes, each about 1cm (½in) across, into the 'body top' panel as shown on the template. For K-9's eyes, cut a rectangle out of the centre of the 'head top eyes' panel so you're left with a small frame.

**3** Bake all the sections of the gingerbread apart from the 'head top eyes' panel for about 12–15 minutes until turning golden around the edges. If the holes in the 'body top' have closed up, enlarge them with a skewer before the gingerbread cools. Leave on the baking sheets for 5 minutes, then transfer to a wire rack to cool. For the 'head top eyes' panel, bake the frame, on baking parchment, for 5 minutes. Crush the red boiled sweet into several pieces and put in the centre of the frame. Return to the oven for a further 5 minutes or until the sweet has melted to fill the frame. Leave to set on the paper.

CONTINUES ON NEXT PAGE ▶

## COOK'S TIP

Position a small battery-powered light behind the eye before positioning the head over the body. If it doesn't stay in place, secure it by wedging in an extra piece of marshmallow or ready-to-roll icing. Take care that you don't break the frame!

**4** To assemble K-9, choose a flat board or plate for serving and stack the gingerbread cakes, one on top of another, on the centre. Put the chocolate in a heatproof bowl and rest the bowl over a small pan of gently simmering water, making sure the base of the bowl is not in contact with the water. Turn off the heat and leave until the chocolate has melted. Alternatively, melt the chocolate in short spurts on medium power in the microwave. Spoon half the melted chocolate into a paper piping bag or the corner of a small polythene food bag and snip off the merest tip.

**5** You'll need to cut sloping sides off the top layer of ginger cake so the gingerbread pieces can rest against it for support. To get an idea of how much you'll need to cut away, lean the side and end sections of K-9 against the gingerbread. Take sloping slices off the long sides of the ginger cake so the gingerbread pieces all meet down the sides with a rectangle at the top where the body top gingerbread will fit. (You might need an extra pair of hands to do this!). Lift the gingerbread away, spread a little melted chocolate from the bowl onto the sloping sides of the ginger cake and reposition the gingerbread sides and ends. Pipe more chocolate along the joins and around the top edges. Position the body top. Chill for about 30 minutes so the chocolate firms up.

**6** Meanwhile, work on a separate board and secure the head side and end pieces together as shown in the photograph. Do this by piping lines of chocolate where the sections join together. Again you might need an extra pair of hands here, or you can prop up the sections with small jars or cartons. Leave to set.

**7** Push the cake pop sticks vertically down through the holes in the gingerbread. Push a marshmallow down over each stick so they rest on the gingerbread. Position the third marshmallow betwen the two sticks. This will help support the head. Continue assembling the head by adding the snout, eye and top sections. Pipe lines of chocolate across the eyes. Secure the fruit slices to the head with more chocolate for ears.

**8** For the collar, roll out the red icing on a surface dusted with icing sugar to a long, thin strip. Cut out a 25 x 2cm (10 x ¾in) length and drape around the neck, pressing the ends together at the front. Secure the green boiled sweet over the ends of the collar with more chocolate. Pipe lines of writing icing over the collar to decorate. For the control panel, pipe a rectangle of chocolate on the top of the body and secure rows of coloured sweets. Pipe further rectangles of chocolate on the body sides. Once you're sure the head has completely set, carefully rest it over the head support so it tilts forward. Store in a cool place.

# THE TARDIS

The world's most famous police call box is, in this case, made of cake in the centre and a biscuit frame. It's specially designed so that the roof lifts off for positioning a battery-powered light behind the windows. This cake is another great bake-ahead party centrepiece. You can make the entire cake, except for the window panes, three days in advance, then add the window panes a day or two before serving as they're liable to soften if left for longer. Cover loosely with cling film and keep it somewhere cool and away from inquisitive fingers!

## SERVES 12–15

**FOR THE CAKE:**

225g (8oz) slightly salted butter, softened
225g (8oz) caster sugar
2 tsp vanilla extract
4 medium eggs
300g (11oz) self-raising flour
3 tbsp milk

**FOR THE BISCUIT DOUGH:**

350g (12oz) plain flour
1 tsp baking powder
2 tsp ground cinnamon
100g (3½oz) firm slightly salted butter, cut into small pieces
150g (5oz) light muscovado sugar
2 tbsp black treacle
1 medium egg
1 medium egg yolk
8 clear orange-coloured boiled sweets

**TO DECORATE:**

350g (12oz) icing sugar
1 medium egg white
navy blue and black liquid food colouring
400g (14oz) navy blue ready-to-roll icing
small bit each of orange and white ready-to-roll icing
100g (3½oz) butter, softened

**YOU WILL NEED:**

a 20cm (8in) square cake tin, 2 paper piping bags each fitted with a fine writing nozzle, a fine paintbrush, a 20–23cm (8–9in) square silver cake board, 1 paper piping bag fitted with a large writing nozzle or a fine star nozzle, and a battery-powered tealight

**1** Preheat the oven to 160°C/325°F/Gas 3. Grease and line the base and sides of a 20cm (8in) square cake tin. Grease the lining paper.

**2** For the cake, put the butter, caster sugar, vanilla extract, eggs, flour and milk in a bowl and beat with a hand-held electric whisk until pale and creamy. Turn into the tin, level the surface and bake for about 45 minutes or until just firm to the touch and a skewer inserted into the centre comes out clean. Turn out onto a wire rack and leave to cool.

**3** For the biscuit dough, trace the TARDIS template (page 150) onto paper and cut out. Put the flour, baking powder and cinnamon in a food processor. Add the butter and process until the mixture resembles fine breadcrumbs. Briefly blend in the muscovado sugar. Add the treacle, egg and egg yolk and process to a paste.

**4** Increase the oven temperature to 200°C/400°F/Gas 6. Line two baking sheets with baking parchment. Divide the dough in half and roll out each half to a 3mm (⅛in) thickness. Transfer to the baking sheets and chill for 30 minutes.

CONTINUES ON NEXT PAGE ▶

**5** Lay the TARDIS template on the dough and cut out four sections, not forgetting to cut out the windows from each. Re-roll the trimmings if necessary and cut out one 12cm (5in) square, one 8.5cm (3½in) square and one 6cm (2½in) square. These will form the roof. Bake the biscuits for 15–17 minutes or until they look cooked and are slightly darker around the edges. Leave to cool completely on the baking sheets.

**6** Beat 200g (7oz) of the icing sugar with the egg white until smooth. Transfer a quarter to a small bowl and keep tightly covered with cling film to prevent a crust forming. Beat navy blue food colouring into the remainder to colour it deep blue. Keep this tightly covered.

**7** Trim 3mm (⅛in) off all the sides of the TARDIS template (you might need to cut out another one if the original has become greasy or you'll mark the icing). Thinly roll out the blue ready-to-roll icing on a surface dusted with icing sugar and cut around the TARDIS template. Dot a little of the blue icing from the bowl over one TARDIS biscuit (you only need the merest scrape) and position the rolled-out blue icing on top. Repeat on the remaining three biscuits.

**8** Use more of the blue ready-to-roll icing to cover the biscuit squares so you have a thin border of biscuit left around the edge of each square. Stack these together to shape the roof. Shape a small piece of orange icing for the roof light and secure to the top of the roof with a dot of icing.

**9** Put the white icing from the bowl into a small piping bag fitted with a fine writing nozzle. Use to pipe POLICE PUBLIC CALL BOX at the top of one TARDIS side. Put half the blue icing in another piping bag fitted with a fine writing nozzle and pipe six square panels onto each side. Shape and position a small rectangular notice to one side and a small white door handle using the white ready to roll icing. Write the notice in black food colouring using a fine paintbrush. Leave to dry out overnight.

POLIC
CALL BOX

**10** To assemble the TARDIS, beat together the butter and remaining icing sugar until pale and creamy. Slice off any domed crust from the cake and cut the cake accurately into quarters i.e. four squares (you'll only need three pieces so the remaining piece can be eaten or frozen for another time). Sandwich the three cakes on the centre of a 20–23cm (8–9in) square silver cake board with half the buttercream. The assembled cake must be no taller than 13cm (5in). If necessary, slice a little off the top. Spread the remaining buttercream around the sides of the cake. Carefully secure the TARDIS panels to the sides of the cake, pressing them gently into position.

**11** Put the remaining blue icing in a piping bag fitted with a large writing nozzle (or a fine star nozzle). Use to pipe lines of icing down the sides of the TARDIS where the panels meet. This will seal any gaps and will set to hold the TARDIS in place.

**12** To finish the windows, preheat the oven to 200°C/400°F/Gas 6. Line a baking sheet with baking parchment. Draw four 9 x 5cm (3½ x 2in) rectangles onto the parchment, turn the paper over and position two orange sweets in the centre of each. Bake for 5 minutes or until the sweets have melted to fill the rectangles (you might need to tweak the melted sweets into the corners of the squares. Don't worry if they run over the edges). rectangles to harden for about 15 minutes until brittle. Pipe dots of blue icing around the rim inside one of the TARDIS windows. Carefully lift one of the sweet panels off the paper and press gently onto the icing to hold the window in place. Repeat on the other three sides. Pipe blue icing window panes onto the outside of the windows and around the roof light.

**13** Rest a battery-powered tealight on top of the sponge cake ready for switching on, then carefully rest the roof on top.

## COOK'S TIPS

This is quite a fiddly and time-consuming bake, but looks stunning and is so rewarding to make, particularly if you light it up! Take extra care when shaping and baking the TARDIS panels. If they're wonky or irregular the cake will be difficult to assemble and more likely to break. For accurate piping it's also worth buying metal writing nozzles in two sizes. One for the white writing and side panels and a larger one or fine star nozzle for piping the windows and corners. Both can be achieved by using a disposable bag and cutting off the tip, but a nozzle gives more professional results. To serve the cake, scatter crushed digestive biscuits around the base to resemble desert, desiccated coconut for an Arctic setting, green-coloured desiccated coconut for grass or blue-coloured sugar for 'space'.

# SHORTBREAD SMILERS

The Smilers were the information system on Starship UK. They were happy-looking figures inside booths. But they could turn nasty in a moment. Bake the chocolate shapes for these angry mouth biscuits and give the family free rein to decorate them with chocolate, jammy lips and icing teeth. And if you want to make your Smiler nasty, simply turn the smile upside-down.

## MAKES 12 COOKIES

### FOR THE BISCUIT DOUGH:
125g (4¼oz) plain flour
25g (1oz) cocoa powder
100g (3½oz) firm slightly salted
  butter, cut into pieces
65g (2½oz) light muscovado sugar
1 medium egg yolk

### TO DECORATE:
75g (3oz) milk chocolate, chopped
75g (3oz) plain chocolate, chopped
tube of red writing icing
50g (2oz) ivory ready-to-roll icing
brown food colouring
6 tbsp reduced-sugar strawberry jam

### YOU WILL NEED:
a paintbrush and a paper piping bag
or a polythene food bag

**1** Put the flour and cocoa powder in a food processor and add the butter. Process until the mixture has the consistency of fine breadcrumbs. Add the sugar and egg yolk and prcoess to a smooth dough. Turn out onto the surface and knead into a neat block. Wrap and chill for 30 minutes.

**2** Preheat the oven to 190°C/375°F/gas 5. Trace and cut out the Smiler template (page 151) onto paper. Grease a large baking sheet. Roll out the dough on a lightly floured surface to a 3mm (⅛in) thickness. Place the template over the dough and cut around with a knife. Transfer to the baking sheet and cut out the remaining dough in the same way. Re-roll the trimmings to make more biscuits. Bake for 15 minutes. Leave on the baking sheet for 5 minutes, then transfer to a wire rack to cool.

**3** Put the milk chocolate in a heatproof bowl and rest the bowl over a small pan of gently simmering water, making sure the base of the bowl is not in contact with the water. Turn off the heat and leave until the chocolate has melted. Alternatively, melt the chocolate in short spurts on medium power in the microwave. Do the same with the plain chocolate.

**4** Use the red writing icing to pipe the outline of lips around the edges of the biscuits. Spoon a little plain chocolate into the corners of each mouth and a little milk chocolate into the centre. Spread the two chocolate flavours together and to the edges of the red piping with the tip of a cocktail stick.

**5** For the teeth, take a piece of the ivory icing and roll under the palms of your hands to a 5mm (¼in) thickness. Cut into short tooth-size lengths and arrange over the chocolate. Shape the tops of the teeth into curved shapes so they look more realistic. Cut and position shorter lengths for the lower teeth. Dilute a little brown food colouring with water to give a thin paint consistency and use to paint over the edges of the teeth using a paintbrush.

**6** Press the jam through a sieve with the back of a spoon. Put the sieved jam in a paper piping bag or into one corner of a polythene food bag. Snip off the merest tip and pipe the jam into the lip area of the biscuits.

"The **SMILING** fellows in the booths. They're **EVERY-WHERE.**"

# JAMMY DODGERS

Jammy Dodgers are Doctor Who's favourite biscuit. Quite apart from eating them – and they do taste delicious – he used a Jammy Dodger to bluff the Daleks by pretending it was a TARDIS self-destruct button. Our version won't explode either, and they are decorated with his famous question mark motif rather than the usual heart shape, though do this if you prefer. If you're planning a Doctor Who party, make these a day in advance and store in an airtight container.

## MAKES 16 BISCUITS

200g (7oz) plain flour, plus extra
   for dusting
50g (2oz) cornflour
175g (6oz) firm unsalted butter, cut
   into small pieces
75g (3oz) caster sugar
1 tsp vanilla extract

**TO FINISH:**
100g (3½oz) icing sugar
75g (3oz) unsalted butter, softened
4–5 tbsp strawberry jam

**YOU WILL NEED:**
a 6cm (2½in) plain round cutter
and a question mark cookie cutter
or a fine scalpel

**1** Put the flour and cornflour in a food processor and add the butter. Process until the mixture resembles coarse breadcrumbs. Add the caster sugar and vanilla extract and process to a firm dough. Turn out onto a lightly floured surface and knead into a block. Wrap and chill for 1 hour.

**2** Preheat the oven to 190°C/375°F/gas 5. Grease two baking sheets. Roll out the dough to a 3mm (⅛in) thickness and cut out rounds using a 6cm (2½in) plain cutter. Transfer to the baking sheet and re-roll the trimmings to make extra. You should have enough dough to make 32 rounds.

**3** Using a question mark cookie cutter, cut out the shape from half the rounds. Alternatively, cut out the shapes freehand using a fine scalpel.

**4** Bake for 12–15 minutes or until pale golden. If the question mark shapes have closed up a little during baking, open them out with the tip of a knife while still warm. Leave on the baking sheets for 5 minutes, then transfer to a wire rack to cool.

**5** To finish, beat together the icing sugar and butter until smooth. Spread over the plain cookie halves and spoon a little jam on top. Position the lids. Store in an airtight container.

# CAPTAIN FLAPJACKS

Captain Jack Harkness, Torchwood agent and sometime companion to the Tenth Doctor, is an immortal – but these tasty little treats won't last nearly so long. With chunks of biscuit, nuts, seeds and dried fruit, all coated in a thick layer of white chocolate, they are just as seductive as Jack himself. Or just great for a family tea or lunchbox filler.

## MAKES 12 FLAPJACKS

75g (3oz) digestive or oat biscuits
50g (2oz) almonds, finely chopped
50g (2oz) sultanas
50g (2oz) dried apricots or stoned
   dates, chopped
4 tbsp sunflower or pumpkin seeds
300g (11oz) white chocolate,
   chopped
40g (1½oz) butter

### YOU WILL NEED:

a shallow 18cm (7in) square tin (if you don't have this tin size, use a similar-sized container such as a plastic food box)

**1** Line the base and sides of a shallow 18cm (7in) square cake tin with cling film that overhangs the sides of the tin. Crumble the biscuits into a bowl and stir in the almonds, sultanas, apricots or dates and seeds.

**2** Put 200g (7oz) of the white chocolate in a heatproof bowl with the butter and melt, either in short spurts in the microwave or by resting the bowl over a pan of gently simmering water. Stir occasionally until completely smooth. Add to the dry ingredients and mix well. Turn into the tin and pack down firmly with the back of a dessertspoon until compact and level. Bring the edges of the cling film over the filling and press down to compact the ingredients further.

**3** Melt the remaining white chocolate as above and spread over the surface of the filling. Chill for 1–2 hours until firm.

**4** Transfer the slab to a board and peel away the cling film. Cut in half, then across into bars. Store in an airtight container.

# JUDOON CREAM HORNS

The Judoon are a mercenary police force. They look rather like upright rhinoceroses – complete with horns. Though if you tried to get hold of a Judoon horn, you'd probably be executed on the spot for assault. Serving chocolate mousse in ice cream cones is a fun idea for a kids' party and saves you having to serve on plates! If possible use waffle cones as opposed to the wafer ones.

## MAKES 10 CREAM HORNS

175g (6oz) plain chocolate, chopped
10 ice cream cones
75g (3oz) milk chocolate, chopped
4 tbsp double cream
4 medium egg whites
1 tbsp caster sugar
chocolate flavour sprinkles
cocoa powder, for dusting

**1** Put 100g (3½oz) of the plain chocolate in a heatproof bowl and rest the bowl over a pan of gently simmering water, making sure the base of the bowl is not in contact with the water. Turn off the heat and leave until the chocolate has melted. Spoon a little of the melted chocolate into an ice cream cone and spread up the sides with a pastry brush. Repeat with the remainder and chill while making the mousse.

**2** Put the remaining plain chocolate, the milk chocolate and cream in the bowl and melt over the heat again as before. Stir occasionally until smooth.

**3** Whisk the egg whites in a thoroughly clean bowl until only just peaking. When the whisk is lifted from the bowl, the peaks should just start to flop over. Whisk in the sugar. Using a large metal spoon, fold a quarter of the whites into the chocolate mixture. Scrape the chocolate mixture out into the remaining whites and fold gently together until no streaks of egg white remain.

**4** Place the ice cream cones in tumblers ready for filling. Half fill each cone with mousse, then tap the tumblers on the surface to make sure the mousse sinks down to the base. Fill each cone to the top. Sprinkle the chocolate flavour sprinkles on top and return to the fridge for several hours until firm.

**5** Invert the cones onto a serving platter and dust with cocoa powder.

# EXTERMINATE-A-CAKE POPS

Although the Daleks themselves are unlikely to invent edible components for their casings, or make their sucker arms and guns into tasty snacks, you can do it for them. Just don't let them find out – or you might get a taste of real extermination. These little cakey treats are fun to make and require no baking. Just allow plenty of time for chilling them after shaping, so they're firm enough to coat in chocolate and finish decorating.

## MAKES 12 CAKE POPS

325g (11½oz) bought or
    homemade Madeira cake
225g (8oz) white chocolate,
    chopped
3 tbsp double cream

### TO DECORATE:

150g (5oz) plain chocolate,
    chopped
150g (5oz) white chocolate,
    chopped
tubes of black and white writing
    icing
silver food colouring

### YOU WILL NEED:

12 cake pop sticks and a fine
paintbrush

1. Line a tray or baking sheet with baking parchment. Finely crumble the cake into a bowl. Put the white chocolate in a heatproof bowl and melt, either in short spurts in the microwave or by resting the bowl over a pan of gently simmering water. Add the melted chocolate to the cake crumbs with the cream. Stir well to make a thick, evenly mixed paste.

2. For the Dalek suckers, take 75g (3oz) of the mixture and press in the palms of your hands into a firm, round ball. Cut in half and place each half, flat-side face down, on the paper. Press a cake pop stick down through the centre of each one. Gently push the cake mixture around the sticks so it remains upright. Shape four more suckers (from two more balls) in the same way.

3. For the Dalek gun sticks, take a 40g (1½oz) piece of the mixture and shape into a thick sausage, about 9cm (3½in) long. Push a cake pop stick in one end and through about two-thirds of the mixture. Make five more in the same way. Place on the paper and chill all the cake pops for several hours until firm.

4. To finish, melt the plain and white chocolates in separate heatproof bowls as above. Line the tray with clean baking parchment. Dip one of the suckers in the melted plain chocolate until coated, letting the excess chocolate drip back into the bowl. Transfer to the clean paper and coat the remainder in the same way. Coat the gun sticks in the melted white chocolate. Chill the pops for 20–30 minutes until the chocolate is firm.

5. Pipe two bands of black writing icing around the Dalek sucker cake pops where the chocolate meets the stick. Holding one of the Dalek gun sticks, vertically pipe lines of white writing icing, 1cm (½in) apart, down the length of the chocolate coating. As you finish each one, push the stick into a bowl filled with caster sugar to support the cake pop as it dries. Repeat with the remainder. Leave to set.

6. Using a fine paintbrush, paint the white writing icing with silver food colouring.

"What are you going to do? **SUCKER ME TO DEATH?**"

# TIMEY-WIMEY TEMPLATES

K-9 HEAD SIDES X 2

KOOKIE K-9

PAGE 122

K-9 BODY ENDS X 2

K-9 BODY SIDES X 2

K-9 HEAD FRONT
SNOUT X 1

K-9 BODY TOP X 1

K-9 HEAD TOP
SNOUT X 1

K-9 HEAD TOP
EYES X 1

K-9 HEAD BACK TOP X 1

K-9 HEAD BACK X 1

COOKIE
WHO'S
WHO
PAGE 120

# THE TARDIS

PAGE 126

TARDIS X 4

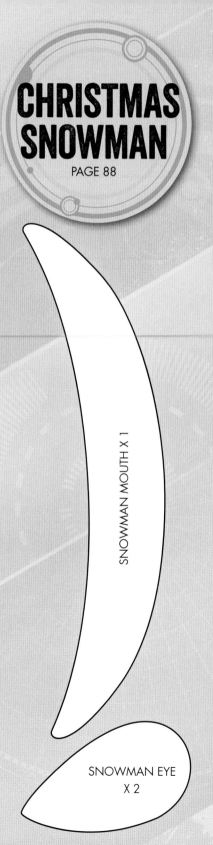

# CHRISTMAS SNOWMAN

PAGE 88

SNOWMAN MOUTH X 1

SNOWMAN EYE
X 2

**CYBERMELTS**
PAGE 14

**SHORTBREAD SMILERS**
PAGE 130

SMILER MOUTH

UPPER EYE RIDGES
X2

SWEET
SILENCE
PAGE 76

CHEEKBONES
X 2

EYE SOCKETS X 2

HEAD

# INDEX

3 5 7 9 10 8 6 4 2

BBC Books, an imprint of Ebury Publishing
20 Vauxhall Bridge Road,
London SW1V 2SA

BBC Books is part of the Penguin Random House group of companies whose addresses can be found at
global.penguinrandomhouse.com

Penguin
Random House
UK

Doctor Who is a BBC Wales production for BBC One
Executive producers: Steven Moffat and Brian Minchin

First published by BBC Books in 2016
www.eburypublishing.co.uk
A CIP catalogue record for this book is available from the British Library

ISBN 9781785940521

Editorial Director: Albert DePetrillo
Commissioning Editor: Kate Fox
Series Consultant: Justin Richards
Copyeditor: Kay Delves
Design: Amazing15
Photography and Prop Styling: Haarala Hamilton
Production: Phil Spencer and Alex Goddard

Colour origination by BORN Ltd
Printed and bound in Germany by Firmengruppe Appl, aprinta druck, Wemding

Penguin Random House is committed to a sustainable future for our
business, our readers and our planet. This book is made from Forest
Stewardship Council® certified paper.